This book belongs to _______________________________

Hello, reader!

I, too, have many unshared dreams and goals in my head, but when I decided to change my life, the first thing I did was write this book and complete it successfully.

Welcome to the second edition of

The Mindset Required for the Teens

In this second edition, I am honoured to deliver to you an updated and extended version of the insights that initially attracted readers. Thank you for the chance to reread and improve my book.

The Mindset Required for the Teens

PRAVEEN BV

Dedication

Actually, I have no idea what to write in this place. Dedication means expressing gratitude to those who support our achievements. So, shall I dedicate it to my parents, who gave birth to and raised me for all of these years? Okay, I dedicate this to my family. Wait, wait, wait—a sudden thought. I also dedicate this book to people like me who are reading it and thinking, "One day, I will achieve great things in my life." I told you I was dedicating this book to you, but how? In this universe, if there is no spectator, the universe does not exist, implying that there is no such thing as a universe if no one observes it. So, until you see it with your own eyes, it does not exist, correct? Then write your name on the blank line below.

I dedicate this book to ______________________

So, I'm dedicating this book to you, as you saw it in your eyes. Are you experiencing anything? But I have a great feeling after dedicating this book to you. Since I was a child, I have been unable to accept things as they are told. I used to ask more questions; if the answer did not satisfy me, I would ask more questions, but after a certain point, I realized that the people would not have answers to my questions, so I would search for them myself. This is one of my habits; you can have different habits and hobbies as well. People will like you if you are one of them, while others will dislike you if you are not. However, this is only up to a certain level. The habit of asking questions from childhood to the present made me to write this book. Finally, I dedicate this book to those who think differently; as I say this, Steve Jobs' saying comes to mind.

"Here's to the crazy ones. The misfits, the rebels, the troublemakers, the round pegs in the square holes, the ones who see things differently. They're not fond of rules, and they have no respect for the status quo. You can quote them, disagree with them, glorify or vilify them. About the only thing you can't do is ignore them. Because they change things - they push the human race forward. And while some may see them as the crazy ones, we see genius. Because the people who are crazy enough to think they can change the world, are the ones who do.

CONTENTS

Preface

Some people save money for years, then after marriage, they build a nice house and pay for it until they are old, and then when they retire, they pay off the loan for the house. At the same time, some people at a young age have created enormous wealth with their minds, and even if they stop working at that age, they will not need to work again until they die.

Everyone is born equal, but their circumstances and choices separate one person from another. To put it simply, we are building a house in our old age, while others are becoming millionaires in their youth. Only this way of thinking changed my life in ways I never imagined, which is why I wrote this book.

When I was 16, I was watching videos on YouTube to gather information for my YouTube channel, I came across a video about money and entrepreneurship that had been uploaded on the channel "Rishipedia". After seeing what was in that video, my perspective on the world shifted completely.

After learning all of this, I began to reflect on the mindset I had developed over the years. Looking back on that incident, I'm very grateful that I clicked that video. Now that I'm older, I have some knowledge about those topics, but when I was 16, they were new to my thinking and understanding.

All humans are born with the same brain, so why do some people's cars cost more than some could ever earn in their lifetime? Why do car companies quote prices that exceed some people's lifetime wealth?

After considering all of these factors, super wealthy people figured out something about the world that I don't yet understand. But once I knew all of this, my perspective shifted dramatically. I can no longer see things the way I did before. Those thoughts haunted me wherever I went.

Until now, I've said that those things changed my mindset, but I haven't specified what it was. So, what is that thing?

Take your time and make a guess.

That is, the people who solve the most problems will become rich. If you already knew this, congratulations, because I didn't know at that age. For some of you, knowing now will pique your interest.

I wondered why no one had told me these things. After feeling frustrated, I started learning more about what I needed to know about this. To be honest, I began to learn about money and the people who earned it the most.

Don't think of me as someone who is greedy for money. What I mean is that these concepts were unfamiliar to me when I first learned them. I became curious about things that were unfamiliar to me. So, the period of my learning from 2020 to 2021 was a wonderful time in my life. I wished to share what I had learned with people my age.

So, reader, thank you for starting to read my book.

The majority of today's youth believe that I am too

young to plan for my future. At this age, only youth are more active and energetic. They can experiment and gain experience. At the same time, if your decisions fail, you have enough time to rebuild the ones that did not go as planned. So, it is important to cultivate the right mindset. Who knows, you might be the CEO of your company, and the people you studied with may be employees. Do you think it will happen? The answer is absolutely yes.

You will lead a far better life if you understand this simple fact. That is, no one or nothing is waiting for you, and nothing is permanent, including you and me.

This was how most people live their lives. Eat, sleep, go to work, and look forward to the weekend. This is the way of life for the majority of people. Living in such circumstances is not the fault of anyone because everyone's situation and life are unique.

People need freedom from the machinery lifestyle. To break the chain, they require money, and in order to earn money, people must go to work, so they become trapped in this lifestyle loop.

However, the equation for wealthy people is completely different. You will benefit from being able to give to others. If you provide a service or product to someone in need, you will receive a byproduct known as money. If you are able to solve people's problems, your value will increase.

People who have more value can only become wealthy. It may appear strange to you now, but don't worry, you'll understand as you read this book because

I was your age at the time. If you have read this far into the preface, then be ready to learn about the events that changed my mind and life.

Data as of 22.04.2024

USD	INR
$1 (One)	≈ ₹83
$10 (Ten)	≈ ₹833
$100 (Hundred)	≈ ₹8,333
$1,000 (One thousand)	≈ ₹83,330
$10,000 (Ten thousand)	≈ ₹833,300
$100,000 (Hundred thousand)	≈ ₹8,333,000
$1,000,000 (One million)	≈ ₹83,330,000 (approximately ₹8.3 crores)
$10,000,000 (Ten million)	≈ ₹833,300,000 (approximately ₹83 crores)
$100,000,000 (Hundred million)	≈ ₹8,333,000,000 (approximately ₹830 crores)
$1,000,000,000 (One billion)	≈ ₹83,330,000,000 (approximately ₹8,300 crores)

This Will Reconstruct Your Mindset

In today's society, education is regarded as the most valuable resource. The heights we reach in life are determined by what we do with what we learn. If we live our lives based on the words of others, we will only get to a certain point; however, if we think outside the box of what is being told to us, we will discover how many possibilities exist and achieve them.

Nobody can stop us from thinking about different ideas and experiencing new things; we have the freedom to do so, but why aren't some of us? Did you try new things and think outside the box? Well, that is what you will do from now on.

Throughout our childhood, society teaches us everything. After we grow up, we learn everything from society. Everyone's life is a journey of discovery, which includes the things we do on a daily basis, our thoughts, and everything else we do.

Do you think beyond what is being taught to you? I used to think a lot about what people told me. I am at my house; my house is on a street; that street is in a city; that city is in Tamil Nadu; Tamil Nadu is in India; India is in Asia; Asis is on Earth; Earth is in the Solar System; the Solar System is in the Milky Way Galaxy; the Milky Way is one of many other galaxies; all of this is referred to as the Universe; there is also a Multiverse theory, but is there anything else after that? If it exists, why haven't we discovered it yet? Why are some things beyond our understanding? Oh, I apologize for getting off topic a little.

So, these are some natural questions that arise in the human brain. I had another thought along these lines.

During my childhood, I attended school for 14 years. After finishing school, I go to college for four years, if I get a placement offer, I go to a job, then I switch jobs if I don't like them, I pay my financial bills, then I build a house because of peer pressure, then I pay a loan amount until my old age, after which I get older and live in that house for a few years before dying. Who knows, maybe I die tomorrow; no one knows what happens. So, I lived my life to contribute to someone else's life, and I died.

But what have I really done with my life? I used to ask myself. What have I contributed to society if I continue to live my life in this way? What did I do to advance the human race and life? When I ask these questions to myself, my mind tells me that you did nothing but live your life for personal fulfilment. If I have only thought about myself and my family since I was born, what will happen if everyone else does the same? I learned a valuable lesson from the universe after asking these questions. That is, in order to receive something, one must first give something.

Have you ever thought about how money works? Think about this: for most people, the amount of time they devote equals to the amount of money they earn.

Wealthy people have a different financial equation. Poor and middle-class people would never think of this because their duties and inflation kept them impoverished, and this circle keeps people from looking around the world, particularly at how money works.

If you ask a child and an adult the same question, I am extremely happy today and would like to offer you some money; how much do you want? The adult will respond with a number based on their circumstances and commitments, while the child will respond with an indirect form of happiness that can be obtained through money, such as toys, candies, or something else; whatever they ask for does not matter; there will be some indirect need for money.

Rich people want to become more wealthier, and poor people want to become richer. "Hey buddy, I already have enough money, so don't give me any," you're less likely to hear these statements from people who have desires and have been caught in the loop because they need money.

Most parents want to send their children to a good college, so they ask their relatives and friends to recommend some institutions with a good placement record. According to them, a good college is one where more companies come to hire skilled students with a high LPA because students need to make money after graduation.

When you are not wealthy, people may notice your appearance, clothing, degree, and type of work, but if you are wealthy, they simply believe you are more capable of doing things they cannot. People will not notice your appearance or degree.

Have you considered this? We rarely use some of the subjects in our daily lives, despite having studied them for 2 to 3 years in schools and colleges, because even if we do not directly apply those principles, we may use them indirectly in our lives somewhere. However, we learn very little about money in schools and colleges, which shapes our lives.

When asked what they want to be when they grow up, schoolboys typically say they want to be doctors, scientists, pilots, and so on. He also says, "I want a huge house with a garden and a swimming pool, or a huge mansion with luxury cars and racing bikes," but if you ask him the same question in college, his answer changes. Can you guess his response?

He will say, "I want to work for big companies like Google, Microsoft, Apple, Amazon, and TCS..." Alternatively, my friends and I were planning to launch a startup using our idea, so we'll see.

If you ask the same boy the same question four years later, he will say, "I'm not sure; those companies did not select me during my placement period in college, so now I'm looking for any jobs that match my qualifications. During my college years, I was extremely happy with my surroundings, but now my life has changed; I am constantly filled with nostalgia, my family situations and commitments are weighing heavily on me; not everyone can become rich; it is all a lie; we must be born into a wealthy family to become rich. So, my life has been squandered. All I want now is to find a job and pay my bills."

But I'm asking you and me: will you be the person who complains about his life? We will not be the type of person who complains about situations and circumstances rather than sitting back and observing what I missed and did wrong over the years. And I am confident you will not be that person, because we are the people who want to change and make a difference rather than complain about the past.

"The money you make is the symbol of value you create." – Idowu Koyenikan

Is there a mindset for becoming wealthy that everyone can follow? Absolutely, yes. Your intellectual mind is now curious about the equation.

Our perspective on money

If you look at the top thousand richest people in the world, you'll notice that roughly 70% of them are self-made billionaires. Elon Musk, Bill Gates, Steve Jobs, Jeff Bezos, and Mark Zuckerberg are all self-made billionaires, meaning they were born into middle-class families and worked their way up.

Even though these people started from zero and have accomplished great things in life, some of us still refuse to believe that we, too, can become like them in our own way. Here comes the thought: no one can become like no one, so be the best at your game.

Peer pressure tells you that if you want to make money, get a good job, but most people's jobs are like having a unique life but instead of living it, they give their time to another person or company by working for them. That person or company will pay them based on the amount of time they have given.

This method assumes that if you want more money, you must devote more time and effort to the company by working for them. If you have earned enough money, it means you have committed enough time to a business owner, organization, government, or company. At the ages of 60 to 70, you will have enough money, but not enough time to spend it.

This one hit me hard: Assume an IT employee in India earns around ₹50,000 per month and a nice house cost around one crore rupees to build. This is just an assumption; you can do your own calculations.

With a monthly salary of ₹50,000, it would take 17 years to build a house worth one crore rupees. Saving the full amount of ₹50,000 is impossible. If you spend ₹25,000 and save ₹25,000 for the house, it can take up to 34 years to build a house without a loan.

People usually graduate from college at the age of 21, so 21 plus 34 equals 55, which means you can only build one house at 55. I hope you've done your own calculations. Do you believe this is the best way to build wealth? Definitely not!

I'm referring to the terms rich and wealthy in some places; do they have the same meaning? When comparing what it means to be wealthy versus rich, it's easy to assume they're similar. Both rich and wealthy people may live a posh lifestyle that is out of reach for the general public. The distinction between wealthy and rich is that wealth is more long-term and sustainable than simple riches.

A person is referred to as a billionaire if their net worth is in billions of dollars. For instance, $1 billion USD equals ₹8,300 crores.

- Mark Zuckerberg became a billionaire at the age of 23
- Elon Musk became a billionaire at the age of 41
- Bill Gates became a billionaire at the age of 31
- Jeff Bezos became a billionaire at the age of 35
- Ritesh Agarwal became a billionaire at the age of 27

"We are building a house in our old age, but they are becoming billionaires during this period."

This made me wonder: how did these things work? How do they do this? What are we missing?

Avoid chasing money

Our goal should be more than just money. Each of us has a unique worth, and the world gives us money based on that value. A cricket player on the national team works less than a military soldier, but who is paid more? Certainly, the cricket player, because cricket players have a large market share among the general public.

People require entertainment to escape from difficult situations in their lives, so they dress up and get tattoos of their favourite cricket teams before watching the entire match with excitement. In the context of this scenario, people who watch cricket are the companies' customers, and those customers are their market.

So, crores of people will be excitedly waiting for their team members to compete in the match; at this point, if a player performs well in that match, his salary will end up with at least seven zeroes.

Assume there is a cleaner and a manager in the office. They will both arrive at the office at the same time and work for the same period of time; who is more valuable? The manager is more valuable than the cleaner because the workplace is a market where the manager has completed a management course and has 5-6 years of experience. This is very sad to understand, but it is the saddest truth: if that manager leaves, it will be extremely difficult for that office to find another manager with the same problem-solving skills as the previous manager; however, if a cleaner leaves, the company can easily hire another cleaner quickly. This is why I stated that this is a bitter truth.

Both the cleaner and the manager solve problems, but their value is determined by how many big problems they have solved.

The person who solves more problems will get more value, and the person with more value can become rich.

Now that you understand the importance of value, how can you increase your own value? The solution is to go and solve problems for those around you.

Begin to solve problems

For example, if your family is in debt, paying it off immediately increases your value to your family members because debt is a major issue that you have solved.

In a friendly trip, you and your friends are struck in the middle of your journey due to a car repair; now you immediately call someone to look into that car's problem; finally, you solve that problem; now your value will rise among your friends.

If someone wants to buy something, whether it's electronics, household items, or something else, they have to leave their house and go to the store to check the price, then go to another store to check the quality, which was a major issue for most people 30 years ago.

However, Jeff Bezos has solved this problem for the majority of the world's population. People can compare the prices of various items, order them, have them delivered to their door, and return the products if they do not like them. All of this can be done while we sit on our couch.

So, Jeff Bezos, the man who solved this major problem for crores of people all over the world, became the world's richest person. Google, Facebook, Swiggy, OLA, and Uber are all examples of high-value companies that grew by solving people's problems.

Here is the secret

You may think that if I create another app like Amazon or Swiggy, I would become rich. The answer is no; this is a common mindset. You might ask, "Why shouldn't I do this?" If I do this, I will earn money, so why should I not do it? The most important lesson I learned was to never chase only money. Those problems have already been solved by high-value individuals; therefore, what problem are you going to solve? Instead of chasing money, we can listen to people who are experiencing problems in their daily lives in various ways. Some argue that it would be preferable if it was done, that would be great if that was done. If we have a solution to that problem, we can start working on it.

> *"It doesn't matter who we are, what matters is our plan."*

- When Amazon was founded, they didn't have any stores.
- When YouTube was founded, it didn't have its own content.
- When SWIGGY was founded, they didn't have any restaurants.
- When OYO was founded, they didn't have many hotels.
- When OLA was founded, they didn't have any autos or cars.

So how did these companies rise to the top? The answer is that they solved people's problems. Everyone needs money, but what exactly do people require? The solution is Freedom. They require freedom from the confines of their daily lives. Eat, sleep, go to work, and wait for the weekend; people want to get freed from this cycle. In order to get freed, people require money.

How Far Would You Aim

What is your highest-level goal that you have set up so far? If you have a goal in mind, it may appear to be attainable in your mind, but it may be difficult to implement. It's easy and common to settle for mediocrity and float through life without really pushing ourselves to achieve our goals.

Do you want something in your life but don't know how to get it? You should try something new.

> *"If you want something you've never had, you must be willing to do something you've never done." – Thomas Jefferson*

What does "aiming higher" mean? It is simply pushing oneself to perform better. It increases the motivation to work harder, think bigger, and strive for greatness.

You must aim for the maximum degree of possible; even if you miss the maximum, you will arrive somewhere which is the maximum for many people. Aim higher, explore new possibilities, and give back to those who need it. You always have access to new ideas and perspectives, as well as the opportunity to learn and grow.

The concept of human space travel was unimaginable 70 years ago, but there is a man who has committed to it and made the impossible possible.

I hope you got the name.

"I think it is possible for ordinary people to choose to be extraordinary." – Elon Musk

Elon Musk is a global entrepreneur and the CEO of Tesla and SpaceX. He also co-founded and currently serves as CEO of Neuralink and The Boring Company. Musk co-founded PayPal and OpenAI, and he is the president of the Musk Foundation.

He is one of the world's wealthiest and most successful men, thanks in large part to his exceptional intelligence. He is also a human, just like you and me, but how did he become so intelligent? To see what the metaphorical seed musk became, we must return to the beginning.

Elon Musk was born on June 28, 1971 in South Africa. He was so lost in his daydreams that his parents had his hearing tested because he didn't listen to adults very often.

Musk's parents divorced when he was nine years old, and it was around this time that he developed an interest in computers. Musk created the video game "Blaster" when he was twelve years old. He was able to sell it at a profit to a magazine, which subsequently published the source code and paid him $500 USD in 1984 money, which is still a lot even today, but it was in 1984. After three years, he experienced a rapid growth spurt and began practicing karate and wrestling to defend himself.

Musk worked extremely hard at anything he set his mind to, whether it was programming with such mastery that he created an actual video game at the age of 12 or studying a variety of martial arts such as judo, Kyokushin karate, taekwondo, and Brazilian Jiu Jitsu. Musk went to Queen's University in Canada when he was 17 years old. One of the reasons he left South Africa for college was to avoid the required time of military service in South Africa.

Musk obtained Canadian citizenship, believing that it would be easier to obtain American citizenship as a Canadian in the future. Musk was accepted to the University of Pennsylvania in 1992 and moved there to pursue an undergraduate degree in economics, followed by a bachelor's degree in physics. Musk was later accepted to the Ivy League University of Stanford in California and moved there to study energy physics, but the internet boom was just getting started, so he dropped out after only two days.

He founded Zip2 Corporation with the assistance of his brother Kimball Musk. Elon Musk made his official business debut in 1995. Take a moment to reflect on this: when a person first enters the business world, things would never be the same again. The Zip2 company is based on web software that was created online; with the advent of the internet, it now offers an online city guide to newspapers. During that time, their office was small, and Musk spent most nights there. He did almost nothing but work tirelessly to make the programme as good as it could be.

Elon Musk: "When my brother and I were starting our first company, instead of getting an apartment we just rented a small office and we slept on the couch and we showered at the YMCA and we are so hot up we had just one computer so the website was up during the day and I was coding at night seven days a week all the time."

Zip2 grew in popularity to the point where a division of Compact Computer Corporation bought it in 1999 for $307 million USD.

Do you think he earned a lot of money, so why should he work again? If he thinks this way, Elon Musk's name would have ended there. It will be a simple one-line statement: "A man named Elon Musk founded Zip2 with his brother; the company quickly became so popular that it was sold to a computer corporation for $307 million USD." That's it; this is what would happen if he got there, but Elon Musk's thirst for knowledge and desire to change the world ensured that he was just getting started.

Remember that Elon Musk studied economics and physics in college, not programming or the industry he went into afterward, that is online financial services. He is very interested in the world and constantly reading books and learning new things. His desire to study enabled him to predict what the next big thing will be.

Musk predicted that as the internet evolved, the ability to pay for products online would need to be simplified and more easily accessible. With this in mind, Musk founded x.com with three other people.

Later, in 2000, x.com, an online bank, merged with

Confinity, and the resulting company was renamed PayPal. In 2002, eBay, an American multinational e-commerce company, paid $1.5 billion USD for PayPal. Musk owned 11.7% of PayPal's equity at the time of the acquisition.

Musk was primarily interested in programming at the time, but he was far from finished developing his knowledge and business.

Elon Musk founded SpaceX in 2002 with the goal of leveraging his physics knowledge and commercial skills to build a company capable of exploring space and eventually transporting humans to Mars. This idea seemed far-fetched at the time because space travel was not privatized and was something that governments investigated.

"Smart people learn from everything and everyone, average people from their experiences, stupid people already have the answers." – Socrates

What I've learned from this is to be a person who learns from everything and everyone before deciding what you really need. While the world defines individuals by degrees, the more degrees a person has, the more talented he is, it is not true and on the other hand people are identified by their skills, beliefs, and accomplishments.

Elon Musk has two degrees, but he does not believe they have contributed to his success. Elon was raised on books, and his dedication to them extends beyond his most recent accomplishments. He is also known for his various learning techniques, principles, and exceptional work ethic.

While Elon Musk went to Russia to purchase a rocket for his mission to send one to Mars, he was turned down because it was too expensive, which he couldn't afford because he wasn't a billionaire at the time. He was left with no choice but to build his own rocket.

He asked a man named Jim Cantrell if there was any way to make it less expensive at the time. Jim Cantrell specialized in satellite systems and has worked for a number of space organizations, including the French space agency and CNES.

Musk called him and told him about the spaceship he planned to build and launch to Mars because he thought Jim would be the most valuable person on the journey. Cantrell was intrigued by Elon Musk, despite having never heard of him. However, Cantrell was concerned about Elon's knowledge of space travel and rockets. Cantrell then handed him a few textbooks to read. Cantrell was hesitant and unsure if Musk would read them.

However, Cantrell discovered that Musk had nearly memorized everything in addition to reading it and taking notes on what he read. He has now learned enough to participate in discussions about space exploration and everything related to it. He can now do the same work as a rocket scientist without a degree by simply reading books. Musk built an inexpensive rocket after reading literature, which was later used by SpaceX.

Elon was asked in an interview after SpaceX's launch how he became a rocket scientist without having degrees or coming from a space science background, and he simply said that he read books.

Elon Musk: "I learn what I need to learn to accomplish my objectives and I think most people can do this but they often self-limit. People are more capable than what they think. If you do something like read a lot of books and talk to a lot of people, you can learn almost anything."

According to Elon, the most powerful person in the world is one who applies their knowledge to take action. I learned a meaningful sentence: "Knowledge is the greatest asset; without action, it is meaningless." Some people may be geniuses, but if you do not put your knowledge and intelligence to use, it is meaningless.

> *"Knowledge is like bullets; action is like a rifle. Without action, knowledge is meaningless."*

Be the type of person who applies what you've learned from books to your daily activities. A person was judged not only on how much knowledge they retained, but also on how much of it they applied. The reason I'm saying this is that Elon Musk's journey to build a rocket by reading books clearly demonstrates it. Elon moved from Silicon Valley to Los Angeles after selling PayPal while working at SpaceX. He did this because he believed it would bring him closer to the space business.

Elon Musk surrounded himself with a large number of space scientific experts with whom he could consult whenever he wanted. After moving to Los Angeles, he immediately joined the Mars Society, which was working to colonize Mars, conducting tests, and had an arctic research facility.

If you want to learn something, imagine your brain as water. No matter what colour you put in the water, it will change colour and fit in any shaped container. I learned this from Bruce Lee's words.

> *"Empty your mind, be formless shapeless like water, if you put water into a cup, it becomes the cup." – Bruce Lee*

Similarly, if you read and surround yourself with experts, you can learn anything.

Despite numerous setbacks, including several failed launches, SpaceX has emerged as one of the world's leading private space exploration companies, having successfully launched numerous missions to the International Space Station. SpaceX continued to develop incredible technology, and it is now the company NASA uses to launch spacecraft, as the NASA has stopped manufacturing its own. SpaceX is also launching thousands of satellites into space for a programme called Starlink, which aims to provide fast broadband internet to the entire world.

Elon Musk was not only CEO of SpaceX at the time, but also CEO of Tesla, which he joined shortly after its founding in 2003. Tesla is a company that manufactures cutting-edge AI electric cars. Tesla has become one of the world's most valuable car companies, revolutionizing the automotive industry with its electric vehicles and cutting-edge technology.

In addition to his work at SpaceX and Tesla, Musk has founded Solar City, a company that supplies solar power systems, and The Boring Company, which specializes in tunnel construction and transportation.

Musk founded Neuralink in 2016, with the goal of developing technology that will connect human brains directly to computers. Yes, it is true. Just think about this, what happens when we use our minds to control computers? The company has made incredible advances in brain engineering, which has the potential to change the way we think about and interact with technology.

Measuring someone's IQ is an extremely inefficient way to determine their ability, but it can provide a very general picture of their innate ability to learn. By the way, what is your IQ? Elon Musk's IQ is estimated to be around 155, while the average person has an IQ near 100 and only about 1% of the world's population has an IQ above 140. When combined with his incredible work ethic and far above-average IQ, Musk is someone who possesses both natural abilities and an incredible dedication to hard work.

Elon Musk has overcome numerous challenges and

disappointments to become one of the most successful and powerful entrepreneurs of our time. His company has made significant contributions in a number of fields, including technology, transportation, and renewable energy. His vision for the future has inspired countless people around the world, including me and you now. Today, Musk continues to push the boundaries of what is possible and is widely regarded as one of our generation's most influential and inventive thinkers.

He is constantly learning and works so hard at his factories that he occasionally sleeps there. In 1995, it would have been insane to generate a billion dollars with an online payment platform, and mass-market electric cars would have seemed impossible. It would also have appeared insane to privatize space travel. Musk, on the other hand, refuses to let anything prevent him from learning as much as he can about anything that interests him and then mastering it, whether it's programming, martial arts, electric cars, space travel, or anything else.

Writing a book and becoming an author was my highest goal as a child, but it has now been accomplished. While I'm saying this to you, Nelson Mandela's words come to mind.

"It always seems impossible until it's done."
– Nelson Mandela

Aim higher and strive for excellence; you'll be surprised at what you can accomplish when you challenge and push yourself to do better. Trust me, if you aim high and take action, you will undoubtedly realize your full potential and exceed your own expectations.

You're The Masterpiece

Abraham Lincoln once wrote to his child's teacher to make a request. The answer is simple: "Teach him that nobody in the world is bigger than him and he's bigger than no one." Unfortunately, most people today compare themselves to others, particularly young people. It's common; I've also compared myself to others without knowing the end result.

Young people like us are more likely to be active on social media, making it easy to compare ourselves to others. I believe it is the road to misery and failure in life. I stopped comparing myself to others after discovering a profound truth. You'll recognize it along the way.

We all have the freedom to compare ourselves to others. Everyone can compare their physical characteristics, professional accomplishments, interpersonal relationships, material possessions, and even level of happiness. It is normal to compare ourselves to others on occasion, but doing so frequently can be dangerous.

> *"Don't compare yourself with others, that's when you start to lose confidence in yourself." – Will Smith*

You're watching videos of your favourite influencers on social media, and at some point, you might compare yourself to them, then feel guilty and move on. Again, you watch them and compare yourself to them, and you feel like you've accomplished nothing in your life.

When we focus on what we lack or haven't accomplished, comparison triggers feelings of insecurity and inadequacy. Furthermore, it may cause enmity and jealousy in those who appear to have it all. When I realized this, I realized that my mental and emotional health could suffer as a result of these negative emotions.

Instead of comparing myself to others, I started focusing on developing my own skills and limitations. Be proud of and acknowledge the things you have done or will do to improve your life. Celebrate your achievements, no matter how small they are. Additionally, learn from your mistakes by taking a step back and reflecting and analysing them. After learning all of this, whenever a comparison enters my mind, I tell myself this.

- Each individual is unique and takes a different path in life.
- Each of us has unique experiences, skills, and goals.
- It is unlikely that what works for others will work for you.
- Don't worry about what others are doing; instead, focus on your own trip.
- Do not let comparison steal your joy and confidence.

- Finally, I tell myself that comparing myself to others in life will make me the saddest person on the planet.

Here's a story that I learned and would like to share with you. It's very simple, but it will have a significant impact on you. The story is about an unhappy crow.

A crow once lived somewhere, but the problem was that he was black. He was depressed and dissatisfied with his life due to his race. He was always crying.

A monk noticed a crow crying, which surprised him. When the monk asked the crow why are you crying? The crow replied, "What to do if not crying is really my life. It really is a colour. The black. I'm unpopular with everyone. No one wants a crow as a pet. "Did you see anyone with a crow as a pet?" the crow asked. I spend most of my time in the garbage because no one feeds me.

"What do you want to become if you have another chance? I will make you whatever you choose, and I will fulfil your wish", the monk asked the crow. The crow stated, "If I had another chance, I'd like to be a swan." White is a lovely colour that symbolizes peace.

So, the monk said, "I'll make you a swan. But first, meet the swan. So, the crow approaches the swan and remarks, "Wow, what a colour nature gave you." You look incredible. You must be happy in life. Look at how wonderful and happy you are.

The swan responds, "Who told you that I am happy?" The crow replies, "Are you not?" Not at all, the swan replied. What do I dislike about myself? My colour. White, which is disgusting because it is used for the coffin. Now that both of them had returned, the swan requested a second chance with the monk. The monk asked, "What do you want to become?" One of them said, "Make me a parrot." People frequently keep parrots as pets because they can speak.

Monk replied, "I will, but first both of you need to go to the parrot and meet him once." After much searching, the crow and swan found a parrot in the jungle and exclaimed, "Wow, how amazing you are." What a colour, what an amazing lip and colour combination. Simply amazing. People give you a name. How happy you are in life. "How amazing your life is."

Who claimed I was happy? The parrot said, but Swan replied, "Are you not?" My problem is that I am green, which is a colour that resembles the jungle with its leaves and trees, the parrot said.

So, three of them returned to the monk, begging him to give them a chance. When the monk asked what you wanted to be, the parrot answered, "I want to be a peacock." "What an amazing bird, what a feather, what a colour—when he dances, people take pictures of him."

"Before I make you all three," the monk went on to say, "you go meet the peacock once." They all ran up to the peacock and exclaimed, "Wow, peacock, what an amazing life God has given you. When you opened your feathers, everyone looks at you. People take pictures of you and wait for you to open your feathers because they admire you. They want to see you dance. How wonderful your life is."

Finally, the peacock asked, "Who are you? Who told you I was happy?" "Do you have problems too?" The crow asked. "There's a lot of trouble here," the peacock replied. Crow asked Peacock, "What trouble are you having?" Peacock said, "Listen carefully; there is a sound." The parrot responded, "Yes, I heard that sound."

The crow and parrot asked, "But what is that?" The peacock replied, "It's Hunter, and he's coming to kill me." Is this life? Why would you want to become a peacock? After the hunt, each feather on my body will be removed one at a time and sold to people all over the world and on the market to decorate their homes.

The crow asked the peacock, "So, are you not happy?" Peacock responded, "No, not at all."

The crow asked to the fellow birds, "What should I become?" Who is the happiest animal or bird?

"You are the happiest bird in the whole world," the peacock told the crow. How can the world make me happy? "How am I?" How can I find happiness in this world? The crow said. "Have you heard of the chicken burger?" the peacock asked. Yes, the crow replied. "You heard about the chicken sandwich?" the peacock asked. Have you seen anyone offer to sell crow flesh or feathers? "No," the crow responded. Are there any risks? Who is living a fantastic life, me or you? Which bird is the happiest in the world?

"You, Brother," peacock said to crow.

We never know if we'll be awake the following morning. Nobody pursues you. Nobody has a problem with you. And who is the happiest bird in the world: you or I? So, regardless of who you are, where you are, how you appear, or what you own, you are amazing.

How did that story go? After knowing that story, whenever I compare myself, I use it to inspire and encourage myself by changing my perspective and focusing on myself. You can do it, too. Take insights from those who have succeeded in the field you are passionate about and use them as a guide to achieve your own goals.

Bill Gates is well-known among most people. He paved the way for others by creating a user-friendly platform. It was a revolutionary start from the technology community at the time. I am talking about Microsoft. I learned so much from his journey to success. Bill Gates was a shy, quiet boy who spent hours in his room reading books since he was a child. He appears small for his age. He was teased as a child and grew up to be an introverted, antisocial individual.

His original goal in school was to teach math, but his friend Paul Allen convinced him to pursue a career in computer programming instead.

Think about this: a single person's proper guidance will change your life in ways you cannot imagine. This is why everyone should have strong allies, as they are the ones who truly guide and uplift you.

As a result, Bill Gates quickly followed his advice

and wrote his first computer program at the age of 13.

Bill Gates' parents were upset; they wanted their child to pursue a legal career. So, to please his parents, Bill Gates went to Harvard to study law, but he ended up spending more time on computers. And that was because he was very excited while coding, and law did not excite him.

At this time, everyone has two options. One option is to pursue the career that their parents desired, while the other is to take a risk.

So, Bill Gates took a risk and dropped out of Harvard University to pursue his goal.

Then he formed Microsoft with his childhood friend Paul Allen, but things didn't go as expected. During that time, he faced numerous challenges and obstacles on his journey. Consider how difficult it was to start a software company back then.

Just think how much difficulty he faced at the time. And Microsoft initially struggled financially.

One of these roadblocks was Windows 1.0. Following its release, Bill Gates predicted that Windows would be installed on 90% of all personal computers, but he was mistaken. Windows was poorly received by reviewers, and only 10% of computers ended up running it.

And that was not what Bill Gates had hoped for. At the time, things were not going well for him, but it served as a stepping stone for Microsoft.

After two years of hard work and long hours, Windows 2.0 was released, featuring significant advancements such as the introduction of Microsoft Word and Excel. As a result, Windows 2.0 was a huge commercial success, changing the world with 90% of computers running Windows as their operating system. Following this, Bill Gates became a billionaire at the age of 31 and the world's richest man eight years later. After becoming a billionaire in 1987, he became the world's richest man. Bill Gates has remained one of the world's wealthiest people ever since. He contributed more than $50 billion USD to the Bill and Melinda Gates Foundation. I wonder how many people's lives he has influenced. How many have been inspired by him? This includes me and you now.

> *"Don't compare yourself with anyone in the world. If you do so, you are insulting yourself." – Bill Gates*

Understanding your own game is your life's work. Also, be true to yourself. Believe that no one is superior to anyone else. You are a unique entity capable of accomplishing things that no one else can.

> *"To win big, sometimes you have to take big risks." – Bill Gates*

That is, the best time to brave life is when you are young because you have nothing to lose, literally nothing. Take life seriously when you are young. Do not live your life like everyone else. If you believe you have something in your head, start with what you have and where you are.

Until they face challenges and difficulties, most people have no idea what life is all about. Most people want their lives to be simple. Most people expect their problems to be resolved by the government or their parents. Remember that the sooner you accept the realities of life, the more successful you will be.

I'm saying you should understand the truth, but what is it? It is that life is difficult, and no one will help you overcome your difficulties except yourself. Your parents and the government are also unable to help you.

When I realized this, I began to accept responsibilities, no matter how small they were. The sooner you take full responsibility for your life, the more successful you will be. So, starting now, take on responsibilities, no matter how small.

If you do not appreciate someone remarkable, you will become insignificant. A coach can help you by motivating and pushing you, as well as assisting you in believing in yourself. During my second-grade year of school, I excelled at drawing among my peers. So, my parents joined me in a drawing class close to home.

After a few weeks, I improved my skills. First, I was taught to draw with crayons and colour pencils, and then I was promoted to watercolour paintings. After that, I was promoted to pencil shading drawings, and after excelling at those, I was promoted to oil paintings.

My art master promoted me through each stage. At the time, he noticed all of my errors and corrected them. I most respect him; he is also one of my mentors, guiding me as I progress in art. He not only teaches me how to draw and paint well, but he also explains each and every detail in a painting, such as how to look at and understand a painting. What elements make up a painting? How do colours come into existence? When I learned from his teachings, I realized why everyone should have a coach in whatever they do. From then on, whenever I do an oil painting, I tell myself that this is something no one else has done in all of human history, so do it as well as you can.

I'm not talking about perfection; I'm talking about dedication. Many people have created many paintings, but I believe that the painting I am currently working on is the result of my imagination, and that piece of art is new to the entire universe.

People will undoubtedly enjoy your work if it appears to be exceptional. So, don't think about others before you begin and finish anything. Of course, everyone's hobbies change from time to time, but inside, I'm still an artist.

Similarly, you had some hobbies as a child, and they

changed over time. Your mentors will change from time to time. Some of you did not have mentors in your lives, but you were influenced by many. So go and approach them as soon as possible.

You do not always need to have physical access to your mentor, coach, role model, or whatever you call them. You can read books written by people who have accomplished what you want to achieve. Reading the works of the people you most admire will allow you to follow their principles.

Life is difficult, and most people are unaware of greatness. If your father or mother is not successful, they will be unable to teach you how to be successful, but they will do everything they can to help you succeed in the areas of support, love, and caring. That can only happen if you show them, you are capable.

As a result, you must seek out and absorb your sources of inspiration. You should look for someone who inspires you outside of your field; once you find someone, you will naturally push yourself forward.

> *"Success is a lousy teacher; it seduces smart people into thinking they can't lose." – Bill Gates*

If you want to achieve long-term success, you must be modest. Many people have achieved short-term success because they were convinced that they knew everything. People who have achieved long-term success never stop learning because they understand that if they do not continue to study, they will fail.

"You don't really start getting old until you stop learning." -Bill Gates

Bill Gates once stated, *"I spend a lot of time reading, even after becoming one of the world's richest men for nearly three decades."* He is an avid reader because he understands that life changes every day, and the only way to stay relevant is to keep learning.

I understand that in this digital age and with the rise of social media, it is difficult for young people to select and read books. However, some people who truly want to grow will schedule time for reading, regardless of how much social media distracts them; they are unconcerned about the distraction caused by social media. The books you read can shape your future. Charlie Jones put it this way: "You will be same person in five years as you are now, except for the people you meet and the books you read."

This is true; life has a tendency to simply happen. But it happens because we make decisions. The life you create and design for yourself will be shaped by the decisions you make over the years. According to one survey, only one of the 60 people planning to start their own business right now will ever do so. Individuals, not only in business, but in general, are so averse to taking action that even when they do, the first or second loss sends them back to their comfortable zone.

Do you enjoy dreaming? Do you prefer to spend more time in your dreams? Consider who will do your work in real life if you continue to live your dream. Of course, it's just you. Most people enjoy dreaming. You can't stay healthy if you only eat sweet things. Dream is delicious, and everyone enjoys it. And because action is unpleasant, few people engage in proactive, determined, planned, and persistent actions. Be one of those who take action, no matter how small it may be. Get out there and have fun.

> *"Our success has really been based on partnerships from the very beginning." – Bill Gates*

Bill Gates and Paul Allen were friends at first, and they co-founded Microsoft. Microsoft's first major success came in 1980, when Bill Gates collaborated with IBM, and he has been looking for new partners ever since, including OpenAI and Nvidia.

Learning how to collaborate with others will help you grow and achieve more in life. This is what I learned from Bill Gates, and you are now aware of it.

If you want to be successful in life, do not compare yourself to others. Use your opportunities, be modest, read excellent books, and learn how to cooperate and collaborate with others.

Keep in mind that you are the masterpiece.

Create Your Own World

Do you know about this? The first step toward any goal or accomplishment is to use your imagination. First, how do you know you want something? First, think about what you want. When you think of something, you will imagine a variety of ways to obtain it.

I used to think about becoming an author. I still recall that incident, when I was sitting in class thinking about writing a book and becoming an author. I also imagine that a stranger approach me and says, "Hey man, I read your book and I loved it." Also, I imagined I was on a train and someone near me was reading my book while I sat quietly and watched him.

During this imagination, the teacher noticed me and inquired as to what I was thinking about. I said nothing and remained silent. Today I remember it and am thankful for my imagination.

Every successful person began their dreams, goals, and achievements with a single imagination. They invented something from their imagination.

> *"Imagination is everything, it is the preview of life's coming attractions." – Albert Einstein*

Do you agree with Einstein's statement? I wholeheartedly agree with this. It is true because everything you see in the world today, such as television, smartphones, automobiles, and airplanes, was once only in someone's mind. What is now proven was once only in someone's imagination; what is now realized was once in someone's imagination. The Wright Brothers' imaginative curiosity resulted in the world's first successful flight.

Carl Benz imagined the modern automobile for everyday use in his head. Steve Jobs, a man who made a dent in the universe with his innovations, created apple in his head. Everything you see and experience in this world was once just a person's imagination. Every one of them has faced criticism and had to deal with it because of their creativity.

People must have laughed at them when they talked about their dreams because they were impossible and nothing more than a fantasy. Not everyone will be able to recognize the immense power of imagination, and those who do not believe will simply work for those who do.

According to Joseph Murphy in his book "The Power of Your Subconscious Mind," the stronger the mind, and the stronger the mind with imagination, the more likely you will be successful. The only requirement is to continue craving whatever it was that first sparked your imagination. We have the ability to turn our dreams, visions, and thoughts into reality and can accomplish anything.

For example, you want to be an entrepreneur, but right now those things are only in your imagination, and you keep telling yourself, "I'll be an entrepreneur," but you are not an entrepreneur. When you keep telling yourself, "I'll be an entrepreneur, I'll be an entrepreneur," at some point you will feel guilty for not taking any action, and you will feel stressed. At that point, your subconscious mind will look for a way to achieve it. You'll start listening to people who have problems, because solving problems is the foundation of entrepreneurship. All you have to do is keep imagining what you want and how you will get it. You must believe that your imagination is real and that you are capable of achieving those goals. While I'm saying this to you, Abdul Kalam's words come to my mind.

*"Dream, dream, dream. Dreams transform
into thoughts and thoughts result in action."
– Dr APJ Abdul Kalam*

When you start to discover your inner strength, it will open up an infinite number of possibilities for you to make your dreams come true. When I was 15, I started to trust my curiosity, and something inside me began to push me toward the idea of starting a YouTube channel.

So, I told the idea of starting a YouTube channel to my friends. My friends at the time agreed to join me, and we began planning the type of content. We intended to use documentary type in history, mystery, and educational videos. My 10th grade board exams were coming up in a month, but I was completely focused on developing that channel.

All of my friends who agreed to make videos worked well for the first month. Then the board exam approaches, and everyone, except my one friend, returns to creating content for our channel.

We stopped worrying about exams and started working on the channel. Our main goal at the time was to reach 1000 subscribers and 4000 watch hours so that we could monetize our channel. After 6 months of consistently creating and uploading videos, we finally met the criteria for earning money from our YouTube channel, which was 1000 subscribers and 4000 watch hours. After that, I realized the importance of consistency. As soon as we reached 1000 subscribers, we reached 2000 subscribers in the next one and a half months, 5000 subscribers the following month, and 30000 subscribers in the next six months.

During the early days of this channel, my friends and I agreed that if we earned even ₹1, we would split it equally among the five of us. However, my friend and I, who helped develop that channel, have now earned five figures in Indian rupees. Why am I telling you this? Because when you set your mind to something and put forth your best effort, you will be pleasantly surprised by the outcome. It will be much more than you expected. I didn't expect to achieve much more than I did with our YouTube channel, but I understand that everything seems impossible until it's done.

Steve Jobs once said, "You can't connect the dots looking forward; you can only connect them looking backwards. So, you have to trust that the dots will somehow connect in your future."

I would not have gained 31,000 subscribers if I had

not reached 10,000 subscribers. I would not have reached 10,000 subscribers if I had not reached 1000 subscribers. I would not have reached 1000 subscribers if I had not reached the first 100 subscribers. I would not have reached the first 100 subscribers if I had not uploaded the first video. I would not have started a You Tube channel if I had not imagined So, it all begins with a simple imagination.

If you start imagining what you want to accomplish or create right now, it will begin to outline the steps you must take to get there. You'll begin looking for different ways to make your dreams a reality. When you start something, people will try to mock you, but stay focused on your goal rather than their opinions.

"Keep in mind that if someone tells you that you can't, they are telling you about their limitations. "Not yours." If you achieve your goals, those who accuse you of daydreaming will begin to aspire to be like you.

> *"The man who has no imagination has no wings." – Muhammed Ali*

A person's greatest strength is his imagination. According to Muhammed Ali, without imagination, you get nowhere and accomplish nothing. The person with the greatest imagination changed the world.

Newton did not discover gravity simply because an apple fell on his head; rather, he began to wonder why the apple fell and did not rise. Imagination governs and enriches everyone's life. It is more than just mindless daydreaming; whether consciously or unconsciously, we use it in the majority of our daily activities.

When we prepare for a party, function, or travel, we use our imagination to envision how everyone will enjoy it and what we will eat, but why do we hold back on our most important goals? Every powerful person who has changed or is attempting to change the world started with a simple idea. They believed in their imagination, and you should as well.

This young man named Ritesh Agarwal inspired me greatly. He demonstrates that age is simply a number and that the only limit to success is one's imagination. Ritesh Agarwal, an Indian entrepreneur, founded OYO rooms, the world's largest hotel chain.

Ritesh Agarwal, born in Odisha in 1993, was a student with a passion for technology and entrepreneurship. He grew up impoverished and suffered for 18 years. He did not attend university and was unemployed at the time, and he considered this to be the most difficult period of his life. He was forced to leave his flat with only $0.50 in his bank account.

Then how did he become the youngest billionaire?

Ritesh Agarwal: Money is not what I ever cared about, for me it is always about solving real problems.

In the process of solving problems around him, he noticed that a nearby hotel was always empty, and the hotel wasn't making much money, so he went to the owner and promised to make his hotel banner, change the lightbulbs, change the beds, put picture frames, put room service, and take nice pictures of the hotel and put them on the Internet, and the hotel went from empty to full. We can simply describe these events in a few lines, but they are the result of a lot of hard work and determination.

Ritesh Agarwal: First hotel is always the hardest, when I was able to change one hotel, I was pretty sure I could change hundreds.

He raised money from investors when he was 20, hired 50 people when he was 21, had 500 hotels when he was 22, raised $1 billion when he was 24, and had 43,000 hotels when he was 26 (as of 2020).

Ritesh Agarwal: Many people told me multiple times to go to university, seek help from my parents to make sure that you can do that. I said that this is just not going to work.

Think about this: In six years, a random kid from an impoverished city in India with $0.50 in his bank account became the world's youngest billionaire and assisted 350,000 others in finding employment. This is not by chance; it is a true result to imagination and hard work. He worked at night, on weekends, knocked on doors, begged for meetings, and succeeded despite the fact that the odds were stacked against those who looked like him.

Ritesh Agarwal: I do believe in luck, I believe if you work hard, your probability of being lucky increases dramatically.

I want you to read the insights shared by Ritesh Agarwal at a convocation.

Ritesh Agarwal's words about thinking outside the box and traveling the world to gain more knowledge and ideas for starting a business: I started my company five and a half years back, and today we run the largest hotel chain in India, the top 10 hotel chains in China and, of course, continuing to make more impact worldwide, but that didn't start very easy. In my short experience, I learned one very important thing. At all times, life presents you with two options or opportunities. either a risk or, on the other hand, regret.

I have always learned that whenever life presents you with either of these opportunities, taking a risk is always better than regretting not taking that risk many years from now. So, what I want to tell you is why risking it is better than being regretful about it in the long term.

The first story I tell to you is that going after what you really want to do. If you are in your early 20s, which means that you have very limited liabilities in life. All you have is the ability to dream and go out and make an impact. So, over the next few years, you'll see some of your friends getting better CTCs, but if you really enjoy doing something else, it's okay to let that be and not be the top CTC candidate.

You will see some of your friends taking world trips on your Facebook account, and then you will feel like I'm having to work 16 hours a day because of my passion. You will have a lot of these sacrificial feelings every week, but remember that in the long term, it will all be worth it.

I had the opportunity to be so ambitious about entrepreneurship, after 11th grade that I used to read about entrepreneurs every day. There were two companies I was very inspired by: Royal Enfield and Indigo Airlines. So, I used to take weekend trains from Kota to Delhi to come and listen to those entrepreneurs. Most of the people around me said that on weekends, life is so good that you end up going every weekend to listen to entrepreneurs whom we don't even know about.

Then I lived in a barsati for a year in Delhi to build really small businesses, most of them are pretty insignificant. Those sacrifices will all be worthwhile because I genuinely wanted to make a difference in the lives of those around me. If each one of us has an ambition, it's okay to sacrifice the usual excitements in life for the next few years to do what you want to do, which means it's okay to take a risk versus being regretful of not doing what you wanted to do.

And 30 years later, you're at a bar telling your friends, "You see this friend of mine who's done so well in his life, I could have also been like him if I had taken a risk." You don't want to be regretful like that; you want to be the person on the photo who's being talked about.

The second one is living a very happy and ambitious life, but with a lot of discipline. Right after I decided that I wanted to be an entrepreneur, I used to read online articles on Tech Branch, Economic Times, and so on about entrepreneurs, and I felt that it would be an easy thing to do: you just choose a good idea, and if you're intelligent enough, it should just become successful.

The third one is something that is very dear to me personally. Surrounding yourself with incredible people. It is my job to bring in solid leaders and entrepreneurs in the company who can build the company one level ahead of me. so that OYO outgrows one individual and becomes an institution with strong leaders. At the same time, you need to make sure that you surround yourself with people who are smarter than you, people who are going to challenge you, people who are going to be honest with you.

I believe that throughout your lives, you will have the opportunity to surround yourself with people who can help you improve; they will be smarter than you and thus will challenge you to think better or people on the other hand, will leave you behind in life. There will be people who will make you feel like you're the smartest person in the room. Always surround yourself with former people, because you are always the average of the ten people around you. Your IQ will only improve if the people around you are smarter and brighter than you. Always strive to get better people around yourself, that will ensure that you grow faster in life.

The fourth one is something slightly more interesting. Travel as much as you can, that travel will be worth it. I have learned whatever I have learnt in my short life by travelling across the world. I was born and brought up on the Odisha-Andhra Pradesh border, in a place where 80% of the population lives below the poverty line, so for me, that was all I knew about.

The first time I came to Kota, I felt that the world was much broader; when I came to Delhi, the world became even larger. For three months, I stayed in a new bed and breakfast, new hotel, and so on, which got me thinking that this is so exciting. World over, every hotel chain in the world is 100 rooms or larger, but world-wide 95 percent of hotels in the world are 100 rooms or smaller, so I wondered why no one is opening a hotel chain that is 100 rooms or smaller because there are so many of them. Then I realized there could be one of two possibilities. One, this is an idea that so many people have tried and failed at, and I am probably the 1000th guy doing it; or second, this is something that nobody has seen, and probably I'm the first guy seeing it, so I should go do it immediately.

As an entrepreneur, you are designed to be an optimist. You always see the positive in anything around you, so I saw the positive that at most I'm going to fail, and if I fail, it's okay because I'm still young and I have very few liabilities in life. After that, when I started the company, I had just one hotel. I had the opportunity to be a Thiel fellow. Peter Thiel started PayPal, and he gives $100,000 to 20 people across the world. When I was there for the first time in California, I saw how big and ambitious people were.

Here I was always told by my father that if you are able to earn a higher salary than I am, you have done very well in your life. But there were people thinking about how to make the lives of millions and billions of people across the world better. There were people thinking about innovation and how to create new things that make a difference in people's lives.

All of these things I learned inspired me to say that just because we're building the company in Gurgaon doesn't mean we can't dream of becoming the world's largest hotel chain, and that's what got us to open in China, and we started the big ride from being India's largest hotel company to hopefully becoming the world's largest hotel company by 2020-2023.

But the point I'm trying to make is all of these learnings, the mistakes that you make, all of this comes because you see the world in a different view than just one city or one location. So, whenever you get the opportunity to travel from the smallest villages in India to the biggest cities in the world, please take it, even if that means that you might miss an important meeting or so on, because the amount of learning that travel brings is incredible.

Always strive for excellence. Never be okay by being number two. And it doesn't mean number one in academics only; you can choose what direction or what segment you want to be number one in. But whatever you choose to be, please always strive for excellence.

Personally, two years after building OYO, a lot of people told me, "Ritesh, why don't you sell the company, take some money, and have a happier life?" And then I went back and I thought, "When I'm 40 or 50 years old, what will make me happy?" Will I be satisfied building something where you can land anywhere in the world and point to an OYO sign and say, "I built this company," or will I be satisfied if I was the person who made some money earlier in my life? The answer was straightforward.

That is the strive for excellence that I ask of all of you to have, because it will ensure that you are always proud of the risks you took rather than regretful of what you left on the table. All of us will get opportunities in our life. Never take two steps back after saying, "I don't know whether I can do it, whether I can't do it, whether I can deliver or not deliver," you should have the self-confidence and belief in yourself that many years from now you will be very proud that you risked it versus regretting it, which means that long term that weekends, those evenings, you could have had a better time.

I'm not asking you to stop having a great time; you should have a great time. But when you are working put in all the effort and discipline that you can behind it. So, you don't have to regret later that I could have worked harder and been the best person in the field where I started working on. Each one of you will create your own stories in the future and end up talking about them many years from now.

Ritesh Agarwal's journey was inspiring, and he exemplifies how imagination and hard work can lead to remarkable success, regardless of your age.

"We do not need magic to transform our world, we carry all of the Power we need

inside ourselves already." - J.K. Rowling

Avoid limiting yourself to a single option. Try to broaden your horizons and expand your imagination; the more you do, the stronger your mind will become and the more effectively you will manage your ideas.

The power of imagination is the secret to innovation, as well as achieving anything you set your mind to! There is a saying that true success comes after a series of setbacks. This is exactly what happened to J.K. Rowling. Let me tell you about Rowling's journey to becoming a world-renowned author.

Rowling's personal life was in disarray, making each day difficult for her. On a train ride from Manchester to London one lovely morning in 1990, she came up with the entire plot for Harry Potter and began writing the story on the train. Unfortunately, her mother died later that year, putting an end to her writing for a while. When she moved to Portugal in 1991 to teach English as a foreign language, her life changed dramatically. She met a man, married him, and gave birth to a daughter.

A few years later, in 1995, she divorced her husband. This was a watershed moment in her life: she and her young daughter moved to Edinburgh, Scotland, to be closer to her sister, with three chapters of Harry Potter in her bag. It was the most difficult time in Rowling's life because she was divorced, unemployed, and a single mother with a baby. She became increasingly depressed.

When things were dark and dreary, she saw the light at the end of the tunnel and persevered through life's trials and tribulations. The year 1995 marked Rowling's rejections and failures in a variety of ways. The Harry Potter script was rejected 12 times, not just once, twice, or five. She was broken, but not defeated. She continued to pursue additional newspapers, and her efforts were rewarded.

The book was accepted for publication by a small publishing company, and only 1000 copies were produced. Soon after, the book received numerous awards, including the Nestle Smarties Book Prize and the British Book Award for Children's Book of the Year. By 2023, the book had sold over 500 million copies worldwide and had been translated into 87 languages. The book was adapted into the well-known film series, which resulted in a billion-dollar commercial franchise.

The novels were enormously successful, becoming one of the most popular book series of all time. Since then, the Harry Potter series has spawned numerous spinoffs, including films, video games, and theme parks. Rowling has become one of the world's wealthiest authors, and she has used her fortune to help a variety of organizations.

J.K. Rowling went from being a jobless single mother living on unemployment to becoming one of the best-selling authors of all time, but it did not happen overnight; she faced rejection and worked tirelessly to realize her powerful vision. It happened due to her imagination.

Rowling is well-known for her charitable activities, particularly the establishment of the Volant Charitable Trust, which helps underprivileged children in Scotland. I hope you have come to understand how her journey exemplifies how imagination, perseverance, and hard work can lead to great success. Your imagination will get you where you want to go, but only if you believe it.

Remember that no one will believe in or support your goals unless you do something for yourself.

Do You Have A Vision

A vision is a mental image of the future that you can see clearly before it becomes a reality. Ordinary people have hopes, whereas leaders are said to have vision. Will you become a leader or just a regular person?

Leaders practice thinking backwards from the future. They project many years into the future and then glance around to see what it will look like; they take a mental voyage 5 or 10 years ahead and imagine achieving all of their objectives. They then return to the present, as if gazing from the top of a tall mountain down to where they are standing in the valley, and consider the road that will take them to where they want to be in the future.

You have imagined something in your mind, but we eventually forget about our dreams. So, what can you do to ensure that you continue to see your dreams? You need to have a vision from now on. The only thing worse than being blind is having eyes but no vision. Where there is no vision there is no hope, so have vision for your dreams in life.

There are no successful people who lack vision. It exists within all of us. Each of us has a unique vision. In terms of vision, I cannot see what you see, and you cannot see what I see. If you see a path and believe in it, it is your responsibility to show and prove it to others, rather than simply telling them about it. Look deeply into your heart. What is your vision? Who do you want to be? Where do you want to go? What is the burning desire, goal, or dream in your heart. Once you've answered the above questions, you'll have a clear vision of your dreams.

It is true that when you work for your goal, when you are on the right track, you will face roadblocks, setbacks, and failures. These things will try to derail you, but your vision will give you the energy to overcome them.

Of course, you are aware of Amazon, but are you familiar with Jeff Bezos, the company's founder?

> *"You can have a job, or you can have a career, or you can have calling. And if you can somehow figure out how to have a calling, you've hit the jackpot because that's the big deal." – Jeff Bezos*

Jeff Bezos became a billionaire after starting Amazon. Amazon has since become one of the world's most profitable companies. It started as an online bookstore and has since grown into an e-commerce behemoth.

Jeff Bezos' parents were still in their teens when he was born, and his father was not an ideal father or spouse. So, they separated after 17 months, his mother remarried, and her new husband adopted Jeff. As a child, Jeff enjoyed disassembling and reassembling things; he even dismantled his own cot with a screwdriver. He spent his summers as a child on his grandparents' ranch, where he did variety of tasks.

During high school, he helped with windmill repair, animal vaccination, and a variety of other projects. He also worked at McDonald's, where he flipped burgers in the back, but that wasn't all he learned; this job taught him everything he needed to know about customer service, working under pressure, and the value of a good manager.

Jeff Bezos: "If you take your job seriously, you may develop responsibility in any career. Working at McDonald's teaches me a lot of things that I don't learn in school. I've practically learnt everything there is to know about customer service."

He was an excellent student, so after graduating from high school, he enrolled in college to study theoretical physics, but things were not going well for him. He couldn't keep up with the other students and struggled with math; despite being a bright young man, it was simply too difficult for him. He once wasted three hours on a math problem, only to have it solved in one minute by a college student. He realized then that he would never be a brilliant theoretical physicist.

So, after graduating from college, he made the life-altering decision to change his major to computer science. Jeff Bezos worked in a variety of fields, but in the early 1990s, when the internet was rapidly expanding, he saw it as an opportunity he couldn't pass up, so he resigned from his high-paying job to sell books online, and everyone thought he was insane, despite knowing there was a 70% chance it would fail, but he didn't seem to mind.

He had the idea to create a massive digital bookstore called Amazon, and the company began in his garage. After six years, Amazon.com had grown into a multibillion-dollar business, and Jeff Bezos was named Person of the Year.

Jeff Bezos: "I didn't think I'd regret trying and failing, and I suspected I would always be haunted by the decision to not try it all."

Amazon began as an online book marketplace but has since expanded to offer almost anything imaginable, and Jeff Bezos is now the world's richest person. However, Amazon has failed several times since its inception, costing billions of dollars. Jeff Bezos shares his journey from Amazon's inception; those words inspired me and I want you to read them as well.

Words of Jeff Bezos: I was working at a financial firm in New York City with a bunch of very smart people, and I had a brilliant boss I much admired. I went to my boss and told him I was going to start a company selling books on the internet. He took me for a long walk-through Central Park, listened carefully, and finally said, "That sounds like a really good idea," but it would be an even better idea for someone who didn't already have a good job.

Do something you're very passionate about rather than chasing what's the hot topic of the day. Seen in that light, it really was a difficult choice, but ultimately, I decided I had to give it a shot. I didn't think I'd regret trying and failing, and I suspected I would always be haunted by a decision to not try at all. After much consideration, I took the less-safe path to follow my passion, and I'm proud of that choice.

As a young boy, I had been a garage inventor. I'd invented an automatic gate closer out of cement-filled tires, a solar cooker that didn't work very well out of an umbrella, and aluminium foil baking pan alarms to entrap my siblings. I'd always wanted to be an inventor. There's a military phrase that I especially love: "slow is smooth, and smooth is fast," and I've seen that in every endeavour I've ever been in.

You get certain gifts in life and you want to take advantage of those, but I guess my advice on adversity and success would be to be proud not of your gifts but of your hard work and your choices. So, you know the kinds of gifts you get. You might be really good at math; it might be really easy for you. That's a kind of gift, but practicing that math and taking it to the next step could be very challenging and hard and take a lot of sweat.

You can't really be proud of your gifts because they were given to you. You can be grateful and thankful for them, but your choices you choose to work hard, you choose to do hard things—those are choices that you can be proud of.

You can choose; we all get to choose our life stories, and it's the choices that define us, not our gifts. Everybody in here has many gifts; I have many gifts. You can never be proud of your gifts because they're gifts that were given to you. You might be tall, or you might be really good at math, or you might be extremely beautiful or handsome, or you know that there are many gifts, and you can only really be proud of your choices because those are the things that you are acting on.

And one of the most important choices that each of us has, and this just as well as I do, is that you can choose a life of ease and comfort or you can choose a life of service and adventure. When you're 80, which one of those things do you think you're going to be prouder of? You're going to be prouder of having chosen a life of service and adventure.

We have never been in a better place to be alive. I mean, it's just incredible the amount of inspiration that the world generates for me, and I think for a lot of people, it's just insane the amount of change, invention, and opportunity.

Will you use your gifts? What choices will you make? Will inertia be your guide, or will you follow your passions? Will you follow dogma or will you be original? Will you choose a life of ease or a life of service and adventure? Will you bluff it out when you're wrong, or will you apologize? Will you guard your heart against rejection, or will you act when you fall in love? Will you play it safe, or will you be a little bit swashbuckling when it's tough? Will you give up, or will you be relentless? Will you be a cynic, or will you be a builder? Will you be clever at the expense of others, or will you be kind?

Every time you figure out some way of providing

tools and services that empower other people to deploy their creativity, you're really onto something. You know you're very lucky. A lot of people end up with a job, and if you don't love your work, you're never going to be great at it.

As a civilization, we will have so many gifts, just as you, as individuals, have so many individual gifts. How you use these gifts, and will you take pride in your gifts or pride in your choices?

When I first heard these words from Jeff Bezos, something inside me compelled me to pursue something great rather than accept things as they are. What are your thoughts after hearing his words about doing great things in life?

Attitude Speaks

Attitude can make or break a person. First of all, what is an attitude? Attitude – It is the way someone thinks and feels about something or someone, or a tendency to respond positively or negatively to something.

It is one of the most important factors influencing how a person lives their life, and it has the ability to shape the outcome of any situation. Having the right attitude can mean the difference between success and failure, and it may even be the key to reaching your objectives. That is why it is critical to cultivate a positive attitude and apply it to your advantage.

"Attitude is a little thing that makes a big difference." – Winston Churchill

It all depends on how you perceive things and how you choose to respond to them. Your attitude is a reflection of your thoughts and values, and it is the lens through which you see the world. It is the way you interact with and respond to the events and people in your life; it is also about how you think, act, and behave, as well as how you feel.

Attitude can be a powerful tool for accomplishing your goals and making positive changes in your life. For example, if you want to achieve something, you must first find people who have achieved what you want to achieve, and then you will try to speak with them and express your thoughts, which is also referred to as the attitude. It can boost your motivation and determination to take action and make things happen.

"Positive anything is better than negative

nothing." – Elbert Hubbard

Attitude can also influence how others perceive and respond to you. People are more likely to be drawn to and want to be around someone who has a positive attitude. If you have a negative attitude, people will want to avoid you and will be less likely to support your efforts.

"Every wall is a door." – Ralph Waldo Emerson

I learned to see the glass half full rather than half empty. A positive attitude can also help you stay motivated and energized, as well as focus and keep going when things get tough. We always look to successful people for advice on how to improve ourselves, live better lives, and achieve success. However, we can see and learn from them, but the most important lessons in life are often learned from seemingly insignificant things all around us.

Did you learn anything from the ants? I imagine you're thinking about what I can learn from such a small creature. Even though ants are small, their mentality is powerful, and by adopting it, we can change our lives. Think about the last time you saw ants face a challenge and then retreat to their hole to relax: never.

If you try to stop them and they don't care about you, they will find another route. If you block their path, they will climb over or around it, but they will not give up and will continue to look for another route. You can only stop them if you kill them; otherwise, you won't be able to.

Why should we give up when an ant never does when confronted with obstacles or when someone else attempts to stop them? Why are we quitting? When faced with a challenge. The reason is that we do not want to get into trouble. Never give up on finding a way to get where you need to go.

Ants think about winter all summer long. Ants are busy collecting their winter food in the middle of the summer because they are always on the go and are aware that winter is approaching quickly.

According to a proverb, avoid building your home on the sand during the summer. Why do we need that advice? Because it is critical to be grounded in reality. Ants, for example, do not think about summer during the summer, but rather about winter. While enjoying the beach and sun during the summer, keep storms and rocks in mind. What I am telling is, it is critical to be practical and make long-term plans.

Ants constantly remind themselves that this winter will not last forever and that we will soon leave this place, so they remain optimistic and never give up hope that the weather will last. If you face challenges, difficult moments, or obstacles, they will not last long. It will change, and a good time will come.

How much food will an ant gather over the summer to store for the winter? Everything they are capable of. The ant never considers it too early to start gathering food. We have plenty of time, and ants do not believe they have run out of time to gather enough food; rather, they begin gathering immediately. They don't think about how much time they work or what time it is; all they know is that they need to gather food. No matter how many days it is until winter, an ant always has the most faith.

The "do everything you can" attitude is great. Never wait until it is too late or too early to start working on or taking action towards your goal. Start now and do everything you can. Do you feel overburdened by your studies, work, or life? Do you feel that you don't have enough time to enjoy life? You're not alone, however. Many of us struggle to balance work, relaxation, and recreation.

I learned that if you want to live a happy and meaningful life, you must work hard in your youth, regardless of the direction you're going, because you have the energy and passion to make the most of your life when you're younger.

> *"Nurture your mind with great thoughts, for you will never go any higher than you think." –*
> *Benjamin Disraeli*

If you devote your time and energy to productive time management during your early years, you will be able to lay a solid foundation for your future. Working hard will provide you with the resources and information you need to meet your goals and realize your journey. By working hard and investing wisely in your youth, you will be able to live comfortably in your later years. So, if you want to live a happy and meaningful life, prioritize hard work in your youth. It will all be worth it in the end.

We only see eagles in the sky, but do you know what their life journey is? It is very interesting to learn about. They teach us certain beneficial mentalities.

If you want to achieve something in life, be an eagle rather than a parrot, because parrots speak a lot but can't fly very far, whereas eagles communicate very little but can soar very high. A parrot can speak, an eagle has the willpower to touch the sky. The eagle is the monarch of all birds. So let me take you through the mentalities and behaviours that everyone can learn from eagles.

> *"Be so positive that negative people can't stand being around you." – Germany Kent*

Eagles never fly with pigeons, sparrows, or other small birds; they always fly alone. Eagles either soar with other eagles or soar alone, which teaches us to avoid narrow-minded people and to spend more time with ourself because this is when we have the best opportunity to get to know ourselves. I learned a lot by separating myself from small-minded people and spending time alone with myself. That's when I had time to write this book.

Eagles have extremely sharp and powerful vision, allowing them to see their prey from the greatest distance possible. Once they have a clear vision of their objective and goal, they can pursue it regardless of how difficult the situation may be.

The eagle never eats dead animals; instead, they always hunt living ones, and this way of thinking tells us that the past is dead and gone, so we should not pay attention to its rotting thoughts or waste our energy on them. Instead, we should focus on the future and our goals. The past has its own place; don't give it a place in your present or bring them back because, once your past takes place in your present, your past will never allow you to remain in the present, so no matter how horrible the things that have happened to you in the past have been, all those thoughts and memories are already dead and gone, so keep things current.

When a storm begins, all the birds hide and are terrified, but eagles enjoy it and are prepared for battle. Eagles are overjoyed when storm clouds form. Eagles use strong winds to soar even higher, and when they soar high enough, they can be seen above the clouds.

"Train your brain to see great in everything."

Napoleon Hill once said that "Every great challenge

brings a great opportunity with it." So, like that eagle, take on the challenges, learn from them, and seize the opportunity. All of your difficulties will be under your control and overcome the moment you begin doing this and seeing the opportunities.

Eagles usually remove soft grass from their nests to keep their young from becoming comfortable, because if they do, they will remain there and be unable to leave their comfort zone. Although an eagle is a bird, imagine they are aware that there is no room for growth in their comfort zone. The longer you stay in your comfort zone, the more sluggish and uncomfortable your life will become in the long run.

Before trusting, the eagle tests its commitment. When a female and a male eagle decide to mate, the female tests the male's willingness to commit by picking up a twig and flying extremely high. When she has reached a suitable height, she lets the twig fall to the ground and instructs the male to catch it. The male must catch the twig before it falls to the ground, or else he will lose her trust. This method teaches us that we must assess the dedication of those with whom we intend to collaborate before working on an idea. Establishing a trusting relationship is critical.

The Eagle is the species with the longest life span. It has a 70-year life expectancy. But before reaching this age, the eagle must make a difficult decision! In its 40th year, the eagle's long and flexible Talons can no longer grasp a prey item used for food. Its long, sharp beak bends. Its old and heavy wings, due to their thick feathers, stick to its chest, making flight difficult.

The eagle is then given only two options: die or go through a painful process of transformation! The process lasts 150 days (5 months). The process requires the eagle to fly to a mountaintop and sit on its nest. The eagle knocks its beak against a rock, plucking it out. The eagle will then wait for its new beak to grow before plucking out its talons.

When the eagle's talons grow back, it begins plucking its aged feathers. Following this, the eagle takes its famous flight of rebirth and lives for another 30 years. If there is no suffering, there is no gain, which is a lesson we can apply in our daily lives. Many of us aspire to success or change, but growth requires sacrifice, effort, setbacks, and heartache.

So, work as hard as an ant and think like an eagle. Take control of your attitude and turn it to your advantage. Develop a positive attitude and apply it to stay focused, motivated, and on track. And use it to expand your network and influence those around you.

> *"In one minute, you can change your attitude and, in that minute, you can change your entire day." – Spencer Johnson*

The power of attitude is real, and it can make a huge difference. Take the time to cultivate a positive attitude and leverage it to your advantage. You'll be surprised at the difference it can make in your life.

We Become What We Believe

Do you believe we become what we think? It is correct, and I wholeheartedly believe in it. The majority of the time, we become what we think. It's not about thinking something and then acting on it; it's about thinking about what you want and how to get it most of the time.

You will become who you want to be if you have the freedom to fail. Why do you need the freedom to fail? In our society, when we tell our parents and relatives about our dreams, they simply do not believe in, which is perfectly fine because they believe in you when you demonstrate that you are capable; otherwise, no words can convince them. When you start thinking about what you want to be at a young age, you are more likely to have the freedom to pursue your goals.

I truly believe that we become what we think because I am currently experiencing it. I spent most of my 15s fantasizing about becoming an author, and now I am one. So, regardless of what you believe, you will only become what you work for. I believe that the universe responds in equal and opposite ways. If you work for something, the opposite response is the result; if there is no result, the opposite response is lessons, but you will always get something in return.

I was greatly inspired by an author named Brian Tracy. He is a motivational public speaker and self-development author of over 80 books, which have been translated into numerous languages. I'd like you to read the insights I learned from Brian Tracy for people who want to achieve great things in life.

Things I learned from Brian Tracy: This is the great discovery of the great philosophers, metaphysicians, and mystics. It is the foundation of psychology, and the foundation of success is that you are mostly what you think about. So, what do you usually think about? Basically, you create your own life through your own thinking, and your outer world reflects your inner world.

Over the years, over 350,000 people have been interviewed with the question, "What are you thinking about right now?" The top 10% of income earners all responded the same way: they think about what they want and how to get it most of the time. When you start thinking and talking about what you want and how to get it, you start moving quickly toward your goals, and your goals start moving towards you.

The more you think what you want and how to achieve it, the more positive and optimistic you become. You create an energy field that attracts people, resources, and ideas to help you achieve your goals. You wouldn't go grocery shopping without a list. Your job is to decide exactly what you want, write it down, devise a strategy for achieving it, and then work on it every day. Fortunately, you can learn how to set goals. Every time you sit down and achieve a goal, you improve, and it takes less time to achieve the next one.

Now, one of the most difficult concepts for people to grasp is that their entire outer world is merely a mirror that reflects back to them with absolute, complete accuracy what is going on inside. Much of what happens inside is conscious; some of it is unconscious, but our external world is largely determined by how we think, see, and feel about ourselves on the inside.

If you want to change anything on the outside, you must first change something on the inside. Imagine someone looking in the mirror and disliking the way their makeup is applied or the appearance of their face, so they begin to pound the mirror, but the mirror simply reflects what you present to it. So, if you want to change what you see in the mirror, you must first change what you present. Once you understand this, you will automatically rank among the top 10% of thinkers in the world.

The most important aspect of leadership is responsibility. It is to accept responsibility, which means that I am where I am and who I am because of my own actions. Many years have been spent researching the psychology of success and failure, and most studies conclude that there are two major mental barriers that people face.

The first is "Learned Helplessness." This attitude affects 80% of the population, possibly more. People feel helpless. They are overwhelmed by everything going on around them. They believe there is nothing they can do to improve their lives. The words "I can't" are the most common indicator of learned helplessness. People believe that they cannot lose weight, get a better work to do, improve or change their surroundings, increase their incomes, expand their knowledge and skills, or do anything else they desire. They have tried unsuccessfully so many times that they have come to believe that there is nothing they can do to change the future.

The second factor that holds people back is known as the "Comfort Zone." Humans are creatures of habit; they start doing something and quickly become comfortable with it. After a while, they become extremely resistant to changing what they're doing or the situation they're in, even if they're not particularly happy or satisfied with it. They become content and complacent, and they eventually become fearful of change for any reason. The longer they stay in it, the deeper it becomes, until they lose hope of ever changing or improving their situation.

The deadly combination of learned helplessness and the comfort zone leaves a person feeling trapped and helpless, weak and powerless, unable to take control or make a meaningful difference in their lives. But the truth is that there are no real boundaries to what you can accomplish in life.

> *"If you believe you can do a thing or you believe you cannot, in either case, you're probably right."*

Remember that the only limits to what you can do, have, and be are the ones you set for your own abilities and potential. By learning to think big about yourself and your future, you will be able to take firm control of your life's direction and accomplish more in the next few years than most people do in their lifetime.

Everything in your physical world starts with a thought in your mind. There are four powerful mental laws that I learned.

The first is the law of belief.

This means that whatever you believe and feel becomes your reality. If you truly believe that you are destined to be a great success, nothing in the world can prevent you from becoming one. The most important job you have is to change your beliefs on the inside so that they are consistent with the realities you want to experience on the outside.

The second law is the law of expectation.

According to this law, whatever you confidently expect will become your own self-fulfilling prophecy. If you expect success, you will get it. If you expect to be happy and popular, you will find that you are. You are constantly telling your own fortune by talking about how you believe things will turn out.

Positive, successful, and winning people have a positive attitude toward themselves. They expect to be successful in advance and are rarely disappointed. Remember that the best way to predict the future is to create it, and you create your future by how you handle everything that happens to you, whether positively or negatively.

The third law is the Law of Attraction.

This law states that you are a living magnet who

attracts people and circumstances that are consistent with your dominant thought. The more you think about something and become excited about achieving it, the more you will attract it into your life, just as a magnet attracts iron filings. You will attract the people, situations, ideas, opportunities, and resources required to help you achieve your objectives.

The final law is the law of correspondence.

It states that you are always present wherever you go. You can see yourself wherever you look. Your external world of wealth, work, relationships, and health will always reflect what is going on inside you. The laws of belief, expectations, attraction, and correspondence, when combined, are the keys to accomplishing great things in your life. When you start thinking big about your dreams and goals, you shift your beliefs, gain control of your expectations, and activate the law of attraction. You create corresponding changes in the world around you.

Successful and happy people possess a successful and happy mindset. Prosperous and wealthy people have a prosperous and wealthy mindset, and if you adopt the same mindset as other successful people, you will have the same results and experiences in the world around you. Because everything you create in your outer world begins with a thought, the larger your dreams, the greater your success.

It is said that ordinary people have hopes, whereas leaders have vision. The most important aspect of dreaming big is to identify your ideal future vision.

Before you start thinking about what is possible for you, you should consider what you truly want. You dream big by looking into the future and imagining that there are no limits to your abilities.

When you imagine having no limitations, you break the psychological bonds of learned helplessness and your comfort zone. You rise above your current situation and pretend for a while that you have all of the time, money, people, resources, education, knowledge, and experience that you could ever want to be, have, or do anything you can think of.

Here's a great quote: "A thought that is disconnected from emotion has no effect." An emotion that is not guided by thought is simply chaos, whereas a clear thought is accompanied by an emotion, which can be one of desire—I really want that—or fear—I'm afraid of trying it.

You will never stop working, by the way, because knowledge workers never do. They simply do different things. If you stop using your brain, you will deteriorate rapidly.

You now understand what the people at the top are thinking, what they want, and how to get it most of the time. There is a go-forward word, which I believe you will use for the rest of your career. This is the word that set me on a fast track in life. Knowing that will allow you to accomplish tasks faster than the average person. And the word is "how."

From now on, when you want to double something, you're already doing, all you have to ask is, "How?" If you want to achieve more, the question is how? You want to solve a problem. The question is, how? Now, whenever you ask, "How?" Which are what leaders do.

They wonder, how do we resolve this? What should we do now? What are our next steps? Ordinary people are passive. They simply wonder, who did it? Oh my God, what will happen? Is everything over? They're like little sheep running in a circle. Now, when you ask "How?" It's like stepping on the accelerator of your own creative mind, which erupts with ideas like those little lightning strikes or light bulbs in cartoons, each of which corresponds to an action that you can take.

Every time you ask the question "How?" you get ideas. And, interestingly, a study at Harvard discovered that creativity is the single most important predictor of success. Creativity is measured by the number of ideas you generate. And, according to the law of probabilities, the more ideas you generate, the more likely you are to come up with a great idea.

One of the most important benefits is being exposed to a wide range of ideas. Now, when you look at all of the ideas it generates, all you have to do is select one and explain why you want to pursue it. So, what you do is you have a lot of options; it's similar to going to a beautiful buffet. You are not going to eat everything, but you will look at the buffet and choose what you want, need, or can use right now. So, you'll need a buffet of ideas to fill your plate a year from now; you might fill it completely differently, but it's the quantity that determines the quality, and so the more things you do that trigger ideas, the more words you know, the more word concepts you know, the more business concepts you know, the richer your inner vocabulary, the more and better ideas you come up with. So, this is how you become what you believe.

Prepare For Your Goal

In the previous topic, I posed the question, "How do you get ideas?" So, after reading this topic, I hope you have some ideas for work. I also learned some goal-setting techniques from Brian Tracy, which aided me greatly in my journey. These tricks will significantly improve your journey.

> *"It doesn't matter where you are coming from. All that matters is where you are going." - Brian Tracy*

Brian Tracy inspires people to realize their full potential through effective goal setting, time management, learning, and personal development. He advocates for lifelong learning and believes that anyone can achieve success if they are willing to put in the effort and take the necessary steps.

He discovered during his research that self-made millionaires share a number of characteristics. The first step is to develop a clear sense of direction, because you can't hit something you can't see. You must understand your goals in all aspects of your life.

He previously worked for Hunt Oil Company in Texas, which was founded by H.L. Hunt, the world's wealthiest self-made multi-billionaire. At his peak, he owned 200 companies and earned $3 million in royalties per day. And, before his death in the early 1970s, he was interviewed on television by a friend of

Brian Tracy, who asked him, "What are the secrets to success?"

He stated that there have only been two keys to success in my life, which I will share with you. He responded by saying, "Number one, decide exactly what you want and write it down."

The second step is to figure out how much you'll have to pay to get it, and then commit to paying that amount.

There is a quick exercise in which you take a piece of paper and write down ten goals you want to achieve in the next 12 months. At the top of the page, write the word "goals" along with the current date. Write down ten goals you want to achieve, and then ask yourself this great question: If you could only achieve one goal from this list, which one would have the greatest positive impact on your life?

This is an excellent question because it usually jumps out at you and you say, "That's the one." If I had this, it would change my life more than anything else. Draw a circle around that goal, then turn the page over and write it as a heading at the top. Set a deadline for the goal. Make a list of everything you can think of to do to reach your goal. Then start working on your list.

And here's the kicker: do something every day that takes you one step closer to your major goal. The truth is that choosing your most important goal, developing a plan, and working on it every day will transform your life in ways you cannot imagine. It is the secret to achieving your goals. I can guarantee that in a week, a month, or a year, you will be astounded by the difference it has made.

Brian was giving a seminar when a man approached him and asked, "You know that goal-setting exercise?", "It changed my life." The gentleman told Brian, "I was broke, divorced, and on the verge of becoming an alcoholic if someone hadn't dragged me to one of your seminars." Additionally, he stated, "I went through that exercise and chose my main goal and it changed my life." Brian asked, "Really?" He went on to say "Today that I'm worth over $40 million and I owe it to that lesson you taught me."

The only difference between very successful people and the average person is that they believe in their ideas. Ordinary people simply follow their intuition. Sometimes successful people aren't smarter, more educated, or more talented; they simply follow their inner guide.

According to the research, all you need is a 10% new idea to start a Fortune. Most millionaires make their fortunes by improving a product or service that people already use. They do it a little faster, they add a little more grace to what they're doing. If a restaurant has a loyal following, the food may be only 5% different, but the way the people handles it is significantly different.

You can achieve anything in life if you can come up with a 10% new idea. You'll discover this if you fill your mind with information and ask questions about why people do things the way they do. Look for ideas and keep your mind open and adaptable. Remember, all it takes is one new idea to start a fortune. Everyone has an average of four ideas per year while driving to and from work, any one of which could make you a fortune.

This has happened to me multiple times. How many times have you been going about your daily business and noticed a need for a product or service and thought, "I wonder what if I developed a product or service to address that problem?" And then, two or three years later, a company comes out with that idea, or some company makes a million dollars off of it, and you claim to have had the idea two or three years before. Everyone has had that experience, including you and me. So, all we have to do is trust our ideas.

You must practice what top performers do, which is known as "Idealization." You look ahead several years and imagine that your life is perfect in every way. We discovered that this is the first step toward great success in life. It is up to you to have a dream or vision of a bright future.

Here's an exercise I learned from Brian Tracy. Take a sheet of paper and make a dream list. It simply allows you to go wild, so just write down everything you could possibly want. Brian taught this to a friend, and the person he taught was very excited. That person purchased a spiral notebook and began writing, going through the newspaper and jotting down everything he saw that was pleasing.

He finished with 330 goals the first time around, and

by the end of the month he had 500. The interesting thing was that his life exploded after he activated the Law of Attraction and began to attract things into his life such as people, circumstances, ideas, resources, and insights. This began to move him closer to achieving his goals while also drawing the goals closer to him.

The next step toward success is to surround yourself with the right people. There is research into why some people achieve such great success in life. They discovered that what is known as your reference group will determine 99% of your life's success. Your reference group consists of the people with whom you frequently interact.

It's because we are like chameleons, absorbing through our skin the attitudes, opinions, behaviours, dress style, and speech style of the people with whom we spend the majority of our time. When you start associating with winners, you will notice that they usually have a completely different worldview. They're upbeat, positive, focused, learning, growing, and enthusiastic about their work, and you begin to emulate them.

You've heard of the law of attraction, which states that if you change your mindset, you'll begin to attract new people into your life. When you become aggressive about personal development and growth, you begin to meet other people who share your beliefs, and the old groups with which you were previously associated disband, giving way to a new group. People frequently ask, "Well, where do I find positive people who are thinking about success all the time?" You must first become one in order to naturally attract it.

The next key is to refuse to consider the possibility of failure. The rule is that failure does not exist; instead, there are lessons and feedback. You will fail over and over again until you achieve your goals, but your brain has a cybernetic mechanism, which means that everything you try sometimes receives feedback, which makes you smarter, and when you try something else, you receive feedback, which makes you smarter, until you reach the point where you are too smart and stop making mistakes. You begin to do more and more things correctly and fewer and fewer things incorrectly, but you can't get there without failing. One great rule that has been discovered in interviews with self-made millionaires is that they look into every failure for something positive; they say, "There has to be something good in this that I can benefit from," and the surprising thing is that they always do.

Successful people ask themselves, "What can I learn from this that will make me smarter the next time?" Those who seek solutions, which means that you will always find a valuable lesson in the most difficult problem you are currently facing. Here's another possibility: your biggest problem today may be the greatest gift you've ever received because it contains the lesson that will propel you forward. So, if you stop focusing on who is to blame and instead look for the gift within your problem, it can sometimes change your life.

According to Socrates, "the unexamined life is not worth living," which means that a life in which you do not take the time to reflect on your experiences is not worthwhile.

According to Aristotle, "Wisdom is an equal measure of experience plus reflection," and the reason so few people have wisdom is that they have a lot of experience but never take the time to step back and reflect on what is happening to them and what they are learning.

The next step is to develop a workaholic mindset, as the average self-made millionaire works 12 to 13 hours per day and approximately 70 to 75 hours per week.

I will tell you this about hard work: If you have a job, you are expected to work only eight hours per day. Working eight hours a day will only prepare you for survival, and everything you do after eight hours will be for your own benefit. If you only work eight hours a day, you're in trouble because the world is so competitive that if someone else works nine hours, they have an advantage over you; if someone else works ten hours, they have an even bigger advantage.

Every hour you invest after eight is an investment in your future and success. And putting in the hours after eight, whether it's studying, reading, or working, will pay off in spades. It's like planting a seed. When you plant a seed and water it on a daily basis, the plant that grows is made up of hundreds of seeds.

Next, prepare to ascend from peak to peak. You

must understand that life is never a smooth train; it is always up and down; therefore, if you climb a mountain peak, you must descend into the valley before climbing the next peak. So, life is made up of cycles and trends; as the saying goes, life is two steps forward and one step back.

You'll be knocked down repeatedly. You have to bounce, not break. The rule states that life is an endless series of problems. As a result, life will be full of problems and crises, much like the waves of the ocean, which means that each of us is either in a crisis, has just emerged from one, or is about to enter one. After 30 years of research, they discovered that the hallmark of superior people is their ability to respond to a crisis. Superior people look for solutions to all problems.

So, you write down the problem and define it clearly. If you have a problem, you should ask, "Wait a minute, what is my problem? What am I worried about?" Write it down, and the act of clearly defining a problem often leads to a solution, because a well-defined problem is half-solved.

Let's continue with the one goal you've chosen that will have the greatest positive impact on your life. Now, take that goal and write it at the top of a page as a question. For example, suppose your goal is to create a new product that will have a significant impact on your life. You ask yourself, "What are all the things that I could do to build and sell my product in the next 12 months?" Write it as a clear question: if you have a basic idea about that product today, what could you do to turn it into a prototype in the next 6 months? And what could you do in the next six months to finish it completely? Following that, you commit to writing 20 responses to this question. You must write at least 20 answers, such as "Learn product development, learn designing, learn 3D modelling, learn marketing, learn programming, upgrade my skills," or whatever it is.

Keep forcing yourself to write until you have 20 answers. This is called "mind storming." The first three to five answers will be simple, the next three to five will be difficult, and the final ten will be extremely difficult, but I learned this exercise from Brian Tracy, who has given it to people who have gone on to become millionaires. People who have achieved success with this technique claim that the 20th answer has transformed their lives. And if you've ever done this before, it's absolutely incredible. With this simple brainstorming technique, which he refers to as the "20 idea method," more people will achieve their goals. Once you have 20 answers, choose one and act on it right away.

The next step is to become an unshakeable optimist. An unshakeable optimist believes that good things will happen in the future. Brian discovered that optimists have three wonderful qualities. Number one is that they gain more knowledge. As a result, they significantly increase their chances of learning the correct thing at the right time. The second benefit is that they try more things, which significantly increases the likelihood that they will try the right thing at the right time. Number three, they persist. They never give up. Optimists decide that once they have decided to become one, they will not stop until they have accomplished their goal. Do you know that almost everyone succeeds in a different direction than what they originally intended or thought, but they just keep going, almost like a football player running down the field, running, blocking, changing, moving backward, constantly, but never losing sight of the goal?

Dare to move forward in your life, dare to move forward in the direction of realizing your potential; whenever you have the option of staying still and playing it safe or moving forward, move forward not because you will always succeed, but because it reinforces and cements the habit of moving forward.

In some ways, life is very perverse because the more we seek security, the less we have, and the more we seek opportunity, the more security we have. If you're not afraid at least three or four nights a week, you're not working hard enough. If you're not falling on your face repeatedly, if you're not trembling as you fall asleep with your heart pounding, you're not trying hard enough. You are not living up to your full potential. And it's always a little scary on the outside because we all have feelings of uncertainty, fears, and doubts that hold us back, but the brave person is simply the one who moves forward and continues to take risks.

You can't imagine a successful person lacking the courage to face their fears and move forward. The fear of failure, the fear of making a mistake, and the fear of losing money, time, or effort is what paralyzes and holds us back; however, the fear of failure is a habit that can be overcome by the habit of courage.

After studying 500 of the world's wealthiest people, Napoleon Hill discovered that this magical ingredient is the master key to riches: the ability to force yourself to do what you should do, when you should do it, and whether you want to or not. When you develop that quality, nothing is impossible. We'll discuss that in the next topic.

The Most Powerful Habit

During my journey of learning new things for personal development, I discovered that this is the most powerful and necessary habit that everyone should develop if they want to be successful. Most success formulas fail without this magical ingredient. Your dreams and goals, no matter how big or small, fall flat, but with this magical ingredient, you can achieve anything and everything you want, and it's called "Self-discipline."

Jim Rohn remarked that we must all experience one of two types of pain: The pain of discipline or the pain of regret and disappointment.

Success is impossible without the pain of discipline, so ask yourself:

1. Can you choose the pain of discipline?
2. Do you have the courage to give up things that prevent you from pursuing your dreams?
3. Can you say no to friends' party invitations or outing?
4. Do you have the courage to persevere when you feel like giving up?
5. Do you have the courage to move forward when you feel sick and tired?

If you answered yes to all of these questions, you are capable of handling the immense power of discipline. When I discovered all of this, I asked myself these questions. My answers are:

1. I have the courage to face discipline and am

currently experiencing it.

2. Yes, I am willing to sacrifice the things that prevent me from pursuing my dream, and I have done so.

3. I wasn't sure I could say no in the past, but I've gotten better at it over time.

4. Yes, I have the strength to keep working even when I feel like giving up. I say this because something inside me will torture me until I do what I need to do because doing the right thing even when you feel like giving up is better than regret.

5. First, I believed that I had the ability to move forward when I was sick and tired, but when I went through that, I struggled greatly, so I didn't let that sickness take over me, which meant that I began to take care of my body.

However, 99% of people struggle with self-control; if you possess the power of discipline, you are on the right track. You are now a member of the 1% club.

Brian Tracy also explains the various disciplines that people must develop in order to reach their full potential.

The first is the practice of clear versus fuzzy thinking. The quality of your thinking determines the quality of your decisions and choices. Your decisions and choices determine the actions you take, the actions you take determine your results, and the results determine the quality of your life, all of which begin with clear thinking.

According to a story in the papers, Warren Buffett, Bill Gates, and Bill Gates Senior were at a dinner party, and the three of them are good friends, and they were talking, when a gentleman approached them and said, "You know, I was looking at you, and you gentlemen are very successful." What do you believe is the most important quality of success?

According to a bystander, all three stopped talking, turned, and said "Focus." Focus is the most important requirement for success in today's fast-paced world. You can succeed if you can focus; if you can't, you won't. So, from now on, focus on things that really matter to you, such as discipline.

Brian is always amazed when he walks down the street, flies, or drives because people appear to be completely immersed in listening to something; they have devices in their ears and stuff on their cell phone, they're listening to music in their car, and they're watching television. They can't stop bombarding their minds with sensory input, which makes it impossible to think.

As Peter Drucker once said, "You need to take time to think." The rule is that quick decisions are usually bad decisions. Fast decisions, especially those involving people or money, are frequently incorrect. You consider it from all angles, and the more carefully you consider a decision, the better the decision will be.

How many times have you said, "If I had just thought about that a little bit more, I wouldn't have done it. If I had just thought a little bit better, or If I had just taken the time to think, I would have done it better." When you finally think like this? Superior people, through painful experience, learn to take their time when making critical decisions.

So, one of the most effective ways to develop the discipline of clear thinking is to sit alone for 30 to 60 minutes. When you go to solitude to deal with a major problem or issue in your life, this is what happens: you will begin to calm down, and all of your energy and fidgetiness will vanish, and you will simply be calm. It's similar to a bucket full of silty water that will settle down there, and if you leave it there for a while, the water will become completely clear.

And this is what happens to your mind: it becomes completely clear, and after 30 minutes, ideas start to flow like a river through your mind.

You don't think about the problem or the goal; instead, you relax and look out at the horizon, the picture on the wall, a flower, or a candle, but just look at it. This isn't meditation. Simply sit there quietly, and ideas will begin to flow to you, almost like a boat in a calm pond. If you've never done it before, the concept of solving your biggest problem or achieving your most important goal will be crystal clear, and the ideas that come to mind will be brilliant.

The first time you do it, you'll get a result: an insight, an idea, a solution to a problem, or a goal-achieving strategy. The second time you do it, it will be fantastic, and the next time you will get it again. And every time you sit quietly in solitude for 30 to 60 minutes, you will receive ideas that could save you years of effort.

There is another way to think better. Take a sheet of

paper and write down everything that happened. What is happening? Who is involved? Just write it down, and the most amazing thing happens between the head and the hand: sometimes the exact right choice comes to mind; it becomes clear, but you wouldn't have triggered that superconscious solution if you hadn't taken the time to think on paper.

Aristotle was once quoted as saying that "wisdom, which is the greatest of all human desires, is the ability to make good decisions; it is a combination of experience plus reflection." So, reflect on your experiences; the best way to do so is to go for a walk. Simply take a walk where you cannot hear anything. Take nothing with you. Simply go for a walk for 30 or 60 minutes and reflect on something going on at work or at home. You'll be amazed at the quality of ideas that will come to mind.

"What are my assumptions?" is a good way to think more clearly, especially if you're frustrated or having trouble. Am I making assumptions about the situation that may be incorrect? What would I do if my basic assumptions about this work, product or service, or investment proved incorrect? And here's the secret to good thinking: Be open to trying something completely different.

Be open to admitting that you could be wrong and do something completely different; this will open up your mind and perspective, allowing you to see all kinds of possibilities that you may not have considered before. So, clear thinking is the first discipline, and it is practiced by the happiest and wealthiest members of our society.

The next major discipline is that of setting daily goals. Write out your goals; by the way, all goals must be written down. If you don't have your goals written down, they're not really goals at all; they're just wishes.

> *"A goal is merely a wish without any energy behind it."*

So, write down your goals. Write them out precisely and clearly. The important thing is to write your major goals in the first-person singular, as if they already existed. For example, if your goal is to earn some money in a year, write it every day as "I earn that much money in a year," or if your goal is to weigh a certain number of pounds or to live a certain type of life, write down your major goals in the first-person singular as if they already existed.

Starting today, every morning and evening, take about five to ten minutes instead of watching television just before you turn it on; wait a second; I've got to review my progress; and sit down and review what you've done during the day and say, "What have I done right today that's moved me toward my goals?" It is not necessary to think in the morning and evening, but you should take time each day to review your progress; you decide when that time is.

By the way, rewrite your goal every day, review it at night, and ask yourself the following questions: What did I do correctly? What did I do today that moved me closer to my goals? What would I do differently if I could relive the day? If you ask yourself those questions in the next 30 days, you will achieve more than you did in the previous six months because writing your goals down programs them into your subconscious mind. When you program them into your subconscious mind, you create a magnetic field within your brain, which is the law of attraction.

Based on this field of attraction, it brings into your life people and situations that are consistent with your dominant thoughts. Everyone has had the experience of starting to read about a topic, thinking about it, becoming interested in it, and then unexpectedly attracting that topic into their lives.

If you've had that experience before, you can create a force field by thinking about it frequently every time and everywhere you go, resulting in a field of vibration that radiates from you and attracts everything you need back into your life. If you do this for 21 days to achieve your main goals, your entire life will change, and you will notice amazing changes, as I did. If you're not already doing it, give it a try.

The next step is to cultivate courage and persistence. Courage means having the ability and willingness to confront your fears, because it has been discovered over the years that brave, courageous people are not those who are not afraid; rather, they are those who master their fears.

Many years ago, Mark Twain stated: "Do the thing you fear, and the death of fear is certain." Fear and courage are habits that, if you are afraid and think about your fear and back away, it becomes a habit to back away whenever you are afraid or uncertain. If you are afraid and force yourself to confront the fear, it becomes a habit to confront the fear whenever you encounter something you are afraid of, and you will discover that most fears vanish when confronted. So, everything depends on how you handle it based on your habits.

So, here's an exercise for you. Identify a fear situation in your life today and use it as a challenge. Use that as a test case. You say, "I'm going to confront this fear head on, hammer it, smash it, look it in the eye, and deal with it like a car hitting a wall until the fear is gone, and once you've done that, you'll look up and be a different person for the rest of your life."

During the early stages of developing my YouTube channel, I was very shy in front of the camera, so I created voice over content, in which the voice runs in the background while the visual passes by. At some point, I wanted to brand myself on YouTube, so I began creating content featuring my face. Now I can speak in front of the camera without fear. When you overcome your fears, you will realize that nothing can stop you, and that confidence is something you can only achieve.

The next step is to develop daily time management habits. The rule is that every minute spent planning saves 10 minutes in execution, so disciplining yourself to plan your day thoroughly before you begin will save you at least 10 minutes for every minute spent planning, and according to research, it will increase your productivity by 25% to 50%, possibly even double, for every day that you plan. Making a list is a good way to start practicing daily time management.

Begin with a sheet of paper. Again, think of paper and write down everything you need to do during the day. The best time to create this list is the night before the next day. If you do this, your subconscious mind will work on your plan all night, and you will often wake up in the morning with great ideas for implementing it.

Before you begin, you prioritize your list. Apply the 80/20 rule, which states that 20% of the items on your list will account for 80% of the value and thus be the most valuable. This is the most difficult discipline to learn, but it is the key to dramatically improving the quality of your life and results.

You will supercharge your life if you can start every morning with a prioritized list, start with your most important task, and stick with it until it is completed. When you finish your most important task, your brain releases endorphins, which make you feel great. You will motivate, energize, and propel yourself through all of your other tasks. You'll accomplish twice as much on any given day if you start and finish your major task first thing.

The discipline of time management will eventually spread to all of your other disciplines. When you can show each morning that you have the self-control, mastery, and discipline to begin and complete your most important task, you feel fantastic about yourself.

The next discipline is to commit to lifelong learning. Personal development is what gets you from rags to riches; if you are not constantly learning, you will fall behind. So here are the three keys of continuous learning: The first is to read in your field for 30 to 60 minutes per day. Books are the best places to read because they contain a wealth of information that can help you function at a much higher level.

If you are unable to read a physical book, you can listen to audiobooks and podcasts of people who have already achieved great success in the field in which you wish to excel; however, you must do any of these. Brian Tracy claims that he has heard countless people tell him over the years that reading an hour a day has doubled or tripled their income in a year.

The second thing you do is take as many courses as possible. When you take a course, you can learn more in one or two days than you could in two or three years, or possibly even a lifetime.

Here's a true story told by Brian Tracy: "Some years ago, Brian had a dentist, and just before the dentist retired, the dentist sold his practice for around $2 million dollars. He explained to Brian why. He claimed to have attended a dental congress in Hong Kong eight years ago. This is from California; he flew all the way to Hong Kong to attend the International Dental Congress because there were specialists giving private lectures, similar to plenary sessions, on the side. And he went to this session, which was about a specific cosmetic surgery technique that this dentist had developed that no one else was aware of, in which you could basically straighten out a person's entire front jaw so they looked beautiful for a very low cost with a very high level of effectiveness. He returned, and he began implementing this in his practice; people flew from 5,000 miles away to see him. Every dentist referred their family members and themselves to this dentist, who was able to charge whatever he wanted based on what he learned in one session, convention, or course." That is a true story, and while it could be an exception, you never know where the information will come from.

The interesting point is that the more you commit to becoming the best version of yourself, the more you like and respect yourself, have more energy, set larger goals for yourself, and persist. When you invest in yourself by reading, learning, and improving your skills, you are telling yourself that you are a person with a bright future, and it is up to you to realize your full potential. And as a result, your self-esteem, self-respect, and sense of personal pride rise, and you begin to be promoted in all aspects of your life.

The final discipline is hard work; nothing will help you more than developing a reputation as a hard worker. In the studies of self-made millionaires, they said I didn't have better education, talent, or knowledge, but I was willing to work harder than anyone else. The majority of self-made millionaires work 60 to 70 hours per week for years before they break through.

The interesting thing Thomas Jefferson once said was, "Do you believe in luck?" When asked, he replied, "Yes, I believe in luck, and the harder I work, the more luck I have." So, the harder you work, the luckier you get; the harder you work, the more opportunities you have, the more doors open up for you, and the more opportunities you notice.

It's interesting that when you look at an entrepreneurial startup, a business run by someone who is really pushing forward, you'll notice that the business owners are usually the first ones there, work all day, and are usually the last to leave. The business owner even works on Saturdays and Sundays. At the end of the day, the business owners have a beautiful home, a house on the hill, beautiful cars, a beautiful life, vacations, and a boat in the yacht basin, and everyone says they are extremely lucky. No, they are not lucky; they simply work all the time. If you work longer hours, start earlier, work harder, and stay later, you'll get more productive work done in a day.

Every hour of uninterrupted work when no one is present is equivalent to three hours of productivity when people are around to interrupt you. However, life will eventually put you in a position where you want to give up because that is what it is trying to teach you in order to make you stronger. If you choose discipline now, you will feel uncomfortable for a short time, but in the long run, you will reap the benefits and experience freedom, achieving your goals.

I learned from Colonel Sanders, the man who

founded the fast-food chicken restaurant chain "Kentucky Fried Chicken" (later known as KFC), that dedication and hard work can lead to success regardless of age, despite thousands of rejections and setbacks. His name and image continue to serve as corporate symbols.

In 1890, a child from Henryville, Indiana, lived in the USA. When he was six years old, his father died, forcing his mother to start working at a tomato cannery, leaving him to care for his siblings. Life struck him hard when he was very young, and as a result of the difficult circumstances he faced, he was forced to work as a field labourer at the age of 10. He left home in sixth grade, dropped out of high school, and started working as a horse carriage painter. When he was 16, he lied about his age and joined the United States Army. After being honourably discharged a year later, he began working as a railway labourer and attending the local university to study law, but his legal career was cut short in a brawl.

He was forced to return to his mother's house and take a job selling life insurance, but after a while, he was fired for disobeying orders. A few years later, he started a ferryboat business, which quickly became successful. Later, he attempted to capitalize on his success with the ferryboat business by establishing a chemical lamp manufacturing company, only to discover that another company was already selling electric lamps that were far superior to his own.

Despite his difficulties, this man persevered and

eventually went on to work as a salesperson for a tire manufacturer. However, when the company's manufacturing facility closed, he was laid off again. By the time he was 40, the general manager of an oil company asked him to manage one of their service stations.

However, due to the Great Depression, the station was forced to close again. That same year, Shell Oil offered him a service station for free in exchange for a percentage of sales.

He began operating the gas station and serving chicken dishes and other basic meals to customers who stopped by. His pan-fried chicken quickly became a neighbourhood favourite, helping him gain popularity. After opening a legitimate restaurant a few years later and experiencing some success, he began advertising his meals. To his horror, an argument with a nearby rival suddenly erupted, resulting in a fatal gunfight in which one of his employees died. Four years later, he bought a motel next to his chicken restaurant in the hopes of increasing business, but both were destroyed by fire. However, this ambitious man built and operated a new motel with a 140-seat restaurant until the end of WWII forced him to close it once more.

After the war, he attempted to sell his recipes to other restaurants. His recipe was rejected 1009 times before he finally sold his secret recipe "Kentucky Fried Chicken" to the operator of one of the city's largest restaurants. It quickly became a hit, and as a result, several other restaurant owners franchised the concept and paid him $0.04 per chicken. The good times didn't last, either, as his restaurant suffered from decreased client traffic caused by an expressway; he sold it and was left with nothing but his savings.

So, he pursued his dream of franchising his chicken concept across the country, visiting the United States in search of suitable locations. In 1959, he opens a brand-new restaurant and corporate headquarters. He frequently slept in the back of his car, went to restaurants and offered to cook his chicken, and if the owners liked it, he negotiated a franchise agreement. This was in 1965.

After years of rejection, failure, and bad luck, colonel Sander's franchise model achieved great success when he was 75. KFC was one of the first fast-food restaurants to expand globally, opening locations in Jamaica, Mexico, Canada, and the United Kingdom. He visited KFC locations and delighted customers all over the world, traveling over 400,000 kilometres per year. Colonel Sander died at the age of 90, and there were approximately 6,000 KFC restaurants in 48 countries.

At the present, KFC will have at least 29,000 locations worldwide by 2024, spread across 147 countries and territories. Colonel Sanders failed his sixth-grade class, was fired from several jobs, had his legal career destroyed, and was hampered by the Great Depression, a fire, and World War II, but after retiring, he became the world's most famous cook. Colonel Sanders, the founder of one of the world's largest fast-food chains, was many things, but his journey was most notable for its success.

What are you going to choose right now? If you choose short-term pleasures today, you will face the pain of regret and disappointment. Most people inadvertently chose to suffer from regret. However, choosing discipline now, even if it hurts, will pay off later in life. The choice is yours.

Keep Looking; Don't Settle

People's concerns and anxieties may lead them to settle for a life that is less than ideal. Some people may accept a job or situation that is comfortable but unsatisfying. Some may settle for a way of life that keeps them stuck, never pushing themselves to reach their full potential. Again, a reminder: If you want to live a happy and fulfilled life, you must work hard to overcome the limiting beliefs and behaviours that keep you stuck.

The first step toward breaking free from settling is to identify the attitudes and habits that are preventing you from progressing. What makes you afraid to take chances? Why do you give up when things get difficult? What beliefs do you have that limit your potential? You may be able to overcome your obstacles once you understand what is holding you back. Try pushing yourself in new directions. Take on new projects or offers that will push you outside of your comfort zone.

When I say this, Richard Branson's quote comes to my mind: *"If somebody offers you an amazing opportunity but you are not sure you can do it, say yes - then learn how to do it later!"* So, whenever I get an opportunity to work on a new project or something outside of my area of expertise, I say yes, and I figure out how to do it later, and believe me, it works well. If you haven't tried it yet, give it a shot.

Do not be afraid to try things that are out of your

comfort zone. These encounters may introduce you to new hobbies or skills that will help you achieve your goals. Don't accept less than you deserve. Do not let fear, worry, or limiting beliefs keep you from living a joyful and fulfilling life. The advantages will be well worth it.

> *"Your work is going to fill a large part of your life, and the only way to be truly satisfied is to do what you believe is great work. And the only way to do great work is to love what you do. If you haven't found it yet, keep looking and don't settle." – Steve Jobs*

Do you know this man, who made a dent in the universe with his creative ideas? When I see this man's picture anywhere, I feel terrific and get a fantastic sense of inspiration. Steve Jobs (Co-Founder of Apple) was a revolutionary entrepreneur whose innovative vision, creativity, and leadership changed the world.

This man transformed the way we interact with technology. He was destined to leave a lasting impression on the worlds of technology and business. If you want to know Steve Jobs' biography, watch the movie Jobs (2013). I respected the values he mentioned, particularly the one about refusing to settle, and I am confident his journey will have a significant impact on you if you truly want to be great.

Steve Jobs was born in San Francisco in 1955. At the time his birth, his biological parents had no choice but to place him for adoption. Steve Jobs was a clever child, but he was tormented at school and wanted to spend his time alone. Steve Jobs was a highly brilliant youngster, but he disliked the school learning process; he preferred to study in unusual ways, thus throughout his high school years, he averaged 2.65GPA, which indicates he wasn't a horrible student, he wasn't the greatest either; he was average.

Steve Jobs enrolled at Reed College after graduating from high school, but dropped out after six months. Despite dropping out, he continued to take classes that piqued his interest, such as calligraphy.

He didn't have a place to stay, so he slept on the floor of a friend's room and returned bottles for 5 cent deposits to get food, which was one of the most difficult times of his life. He also spent time travelling around India, which was one of the most eye-opening experiences of his life. He goes on a spiritual journey to understand his higher self and practice meditation, and these life-changing experiences help him build one of the most renowned businesses of all time.

So, in his parent's garage, Steve Jobs and his friend Steve Wozniak founded Apple; as we previously discussed, this is why everyone should have strong allies, as they are the ones who truly show you the path to what you want to become. In ten years since founding Apple in his parents' garage, the company has grown from two guys in a garage to a $2 billion company. This is not as easy as you think; we can say it in a single line, but it is the result of years of hard work and dedication. Apple released their first Macintosh computer in 1984, but due to various reasons, Steve Jobs was fired from his own company in 1985. If you want to understand what happened, go see the movie Jobs (2013).

"At 30, I was out and very publicly out; what had been the centre of my whole adult life was gone, and it was sad. I didn't realize it at the time, but getting fired from Apple was the best thing that could have happened to me. The burden of accomplishment was replaced by the lightness of being a beginner again, less sure about everything. It freed me to enter one of my most creative periods of my life," says Steve Jobs.

He even opened his own business. After Steve Jobs left Apple, the company experienced little success and continued to struggle, and with Microsoft's success, Apple was on the verge of bankruptcy. However, in 1997, Steve Jobs returned to Apple and salvaged the firm; the rest is history. Apple became the first trillion-dollar company. Steve jobs words will truly inspire you to do something amazing.

Words from Steve Jobs: I dropped out of Reed College after the first six months, but then stayed around as a drop-in for another 18 months or so before I really quit. So, why'd I drop out?

It started before I was born. My biological mother was a young, unmarried graduate student, and she decided to put me up for adoption. She felt very strongly that I should be adopted by college graduates. So, everything was set for me to be adopted at birth by a lawyer and his wife.

Except that when I popped out, they decided at the last minute that they really wanted a girl. So, my parents, who were on a waiting list, got a call in the middle of the night asking, "We've got an unexpected baby boy; do you want him?" They said, "Of course." My biological mother found out later that my mother had never graduated from college and that my father had never graduated from high school. She refused to sign the final adoption papers. She only relented a few months later when my parents promised that I would go to college. This was the start of my life.

And 17 years later, I did go to college, but I chose a college that was almost as expensive as Stanford, and all of my working-class parents' savings were being spent on my college tuition. After six months, I couldn't see the value in it. I had no idea what I wanted to do with my life and no idea how college was going to help me figure it out, and here I was spending all the money my parents had saved their entire lives. So, I decided to drop out and trust that it would all work out okay. It was pretty scary at the time, but looking back, it was one of the best decisions I ever made.

The minute I dropped out, I could stop taking the required classes that didn't interest me and begin dropping in on the ones that looked far more interesting. It wasn't all romantic; I didn't have a dorm room, so I slept on the floor in friends' rooms. I returned coke bottles for the five-cent deposits to buy food with, and I would walk the seven miles across town every Sunday night to get one good meal a week at the Hari Krishna Temple. I loved it, and much of what I stumbled into by following my curiosity and intuition turned out to be priceless later on.

Let me give you one example: Reed College at that time offered perhaps the best calligraphy instruction in the country. Every poster and label on every drawer on campus was beautifully hand-calligraphed, and since I had dropped out and didn't have to take the regular classes, I decided to take a calligraphy class to learn. It was beautiful, historical, and artistically subtle in a way that science can't capture, and I found it fascinating. None of this had even a hope of any practical application in my life, but ten years later, when we were designing the first Macintosh computer, it all came back to me.

And we designed it all into the Mac; it was the first computer with beautiful typography. If I had never dropped in on that single course in college, the Mac would never have had multiple typefaces or proportionally spaced fonts. If I had never dropped out, I would never have dropped in on that calligraphy class, and personal computers might not have the wonderful typography that they do. Of course, it was impossible to connect the dots looking forward when I was in college, but it was very clear looking backwards 10 years later.

Again, you can't connect the dots looking forward; you can only do so looking backwards. So, you have to trust that the dots will somehow connect in your future.

You have to trust in something—your gut, destiny, life, karma, whatever. Because believing that the dots will connect down the road will give you the confidence to follow your heart, even when it leads you off the well-worn path.

I'm convinced that the only thing that kept me going was that I loved what I did. You've got to find what you love. People say you have to have a lot of passion for what you're doing, and it's totally true. The reason is because it's so hard that if you don't have passion, any rational person would give up. It's really hard, and you have to do it over a sustained period of time, so if you don't love it, if you're not having fun doing it, you're going to give up, and that's what happens to most people, actually.

When you look at the ones who ended up being successful in the eyes of society and the ones who didn't, you'll notice that the ones who were successful loved what they did. So, they could persevere when it got really tough, and the ones that didn't love it quit because they were sane. Who would want to put up with this stuff if they didn't love it? Your work is going to fill a large part of your life, and the only way to be truly satisfied is to do what you believe is great work, and the only way to do great work is to love what you do. If you haven't found it yet, keep looking and don't settle. As with all matters of the heart, you'll know when you find it, and like any great relationship, it just gets better and better as the years roll on, so keep looking and don't settle.

Sometimes people come to me and say, "I want to start a company," and I say, "Why?" Oh, I want to make lots of money. I say forget it; that's not a good enough reason. Most people who have started companies have done so because they want to make lots of money, I haven't seen very many of those succeed. People who come, sometimes they don't even want to start a company; they just have an idea that they want to express out into the world, and they often have to start a company because no one else will listen to them.

So, you've got to have an idea, a problem, or a wrong that you want to right that you're passionate about; otherwise, you're not going to have the perseverance to stick it through, and I think that's half the battle right there.

Let me give you an example: When I was 12 years old, I called Bill Hewlett (co-founder of HP) in Palo Alto; his phone number was still in the phone book, and he answered the phone himself. "Yes," he said, "Hello, my name is Steve Jobs; I'm 12 years old, a high school student, and I want to build a frequency counter. I was wondering if you had any spare parts I could have," and he laughed. He gave me the spare parts to build a frequency counter, and he gave me a job that summer working on the assembly line putting nuts and bolts on frequency counters.

He got me a job at the place and I was in heaven. Most people never pick up the phone and call; most people never ask, and that is sometimes what distinguishes those who do things from those who only dream about them. You've got to act, and you've got to be willing to fail. You've got to be willing to crash and burn. With people on the phone with you about starting a company with whatever, if you're afraid of failing, you won't get very far.

Once you discover one simple fact, namely that everything around you that you call life was made up by people, they were no smarter than you. And you can change it, you can influence it, and you can build your own things that other people can use. And the moment you realize you can poke life and something will come out the other side—that you can change it, that you can mould it—that is perhaps the most important thing.

I was lucky that I found what I loved to do early in life. When I was 17, I read a quote that went something like, "If you live each day as if it were your last, someday you'll most certainly be right." It made an impression on me, and since then, for the past 33 years, I've looked in the mirror every morning and asked myself, "If today were the last day of my life, would I want to do what I am about to do today?" And whenever the answer has been no for too many days in a row, I know I need to change something.

Remembering that I'll be dead soon is the most important tool I've ever encountered to help me make the big choices in life, because almost everything—all external expectations, all pride, all fear of embarrassment or failure just fall away in the face of death, leaving only what is truly important. Remembering that you are going to die is the best way

I know to avoid the trap of thinking you have something to lose. Sometimes life is going to hit you in the head with a brick; don't lose faith. Stay hungry, stay foolish, and I've always wished that for myself. I also wish the same for you.

> *"Your time is limited, so don't waste it living someone else's life." – Steve Jobs*

How are you feeling now? Something different, right? I also felt it. He was an average student who failed in his career, was rejected, fired, and disappointed, but he went on to become one of the greatest visionaries of the twenty-first century. So, whenever you're feeling lost, confused, disappointed, or embarrassed, look in the mirror. You will not live forever; ask yourself, "What can I do to improve my own and other people's lives?" Determine what is most important to you, and never doubt yourself. It does not matter what others say; you have the ability to create the life you want.

> *"The biggest risk is not taking any risk... In a world that is changing really quickly, the only strategy that is guaranteed to fail is not taking risks." - Mark Zuckerberg*

At the age of 19, a teenager with a passion for programming created a social media application that has become almost everyone's natural extension for representing themselves on social media. Mark Zuckerberg, the co-founder of Facebook and one of the world's most well-known and influential individuals, was interested in computers as a child. When he was 12 years old, he created ZuckNet, a messaging application that allowed computers in his house and his father's dentistry office to communicate with one another by transmitting messages.

The family also used this application to communicate inside the home. He was also very interested in making computer games for fun with his friends, and as the years passed, he became increasingly interested and fascinated by computers, and he continued to work and develop programs. While still in high school, he developed Synapse, a music player that intelligently recommended other songs based on the user's music preferences.

After graduating from high school, he attended Harvard University, where he quickly gained recognition for his programming abilities. Soon after, Mark and his friends founded a social networking site that allowed Harvard students to create their own profiles, upload photos, and communicate with one another, and the site was officially launched from his dorm room, signalling the start of Facebook. He decided to drop out of college and devote himself full-time to building his Facebook empire, but this college dropout had a clear vision for his future and believed in the concept he was working on; he didn't just drop out; he had a plan and was fully committed to making Facebook a global platform. By the end of 2004, Facebook had 1 million users; by 2010, the company had 500 million users; and by 2020, Facebook claimed to have 2.8 billion monthly active users; however, this was not as simple as it appears; he was 19 when he founded Facebook.

Many of us struggle to make good decisions because we are afraid of taking risks and making mistakes. As a result, we tend to wait for the ideal time to begin something, but in a world changing so quickly, the only strategy that is guaranteed to fail is not taking risks. How many times can we tell ourselves, "I'm just waiting for the right moment," before it's too late? We may be waiting for the perfect moment, but the world will not wait for us.

It's fascinating to learn about the experiences of those who have already followed their inner voice and succeeded. Finally, I'd like you to read Mark Zuckerberg's words on achieving greatness.

Words from Mark Zuckerberg: I'm telling you that finding your purpose isn't enough. The challenge for our generation is to create a world where everyone has a sense of purpose. One of my favourite stories is when JFK (John Fitzgerald Kennedy) went to visit the NASA space centre and saw a janitor holding a broom. He asked him what he was doing, and the janitor replied, "Mr. President, I'm helping to put a man on the moon." Purpose is that feeling that you are a part of something bigger than yourself, that you are needed, and that you have something better ahead to work for. Purpose is what creates true happiness.

As I've travelled around, I've sat with children in

juvenile detention and opioid addicts who've told me that maybe their lives would have turned out differently if they just had something to do, an after-school program, or somewhere to go. I've met factory workers who know their old jobs aren't coming back and are just trying to find their path ahead. For our society to keep moving forward, we have a generational challenge to not only create new jobs but also create a renewed sense of purpose.

When I launched Facebook from that little dorm in Kirkland House, and telling to my friend KX clearly that I was excited to help connect the Harvard community, but that one day someone would connect the whole world. The thing is, it never even occurred to me that someone might be us; we were just college kids, and we didn't know anything about that. There were all these great big technology companies with all these resources, and I just assumed one of them would do it, but this idea was so clear to us that all people want to connect. So, we just kept working on it day after day after day.

And I know that a lot of you are going to have your own stories just like this. A change in the world that seems so clear that you are sure someone else is going to do it, but they're not, you will. My hope was never to build a company; I wanted to have an impact, and as all these people started joining us, I just assumed that's what they wanted to do too. So, I never took the time to explain what it was that I hoped we'd build. A couple years ago, some big companies wanted to buy us. I didn't want to sell; I wanted to see if we could connect more people. And we were building the first version of the news feed at the time, and I thought if we could just launch it, it could change how we all learn about the world, and nearly everyone else wanted it to sell.

Without a sense of higher purpose, this was their startup dream come true, and it tore our company apart. After one particularly tense argument, one of my close advisors told me that if I didn't agree to sell the company right now, I would regret that decision for the rest of my life. Relationships were so frayed that within a year or so, every single person on our management team was gone. That was my hardest time leading Facebook.

I believed in what we were doing, but I felt alone, and worse, it was my fault. I wondered if I was just wrong—an imposter, a 22-year-old kid who had no idea how things actually worked. Years later, I understand that that is how things work when there's no sense of a higher purpose.

So, it's up to all of us to create it, so we can all keep moving forward together, and there are three ways that we can create a world where everyone has a sense of purpose: by taking on big, meaningful projects together, by redefining equality so everyone has the freedom to pursue their purpose, and by building community all across the world.

So first, let's take on big, meaningful projects. Our generation is going to deal with tens of millions of jobs being replaced by automation like self-driving cars and trucks, but we have the potential to do so much more than that. Every generation has its own defining works. More than 300,000 people worked to put that man on the moon, including that janitor; millions of volunteers immunized children around the world against polio; and millions more built the Hoover Dam and other great projects. And now it's our generation's turn to do great things.

Let me tell you a secret: no one does when they begin; ideas don't come out fully formed; they only become clear as you work on them; you just have to get started. If I had known everything about connecting people before I got started, I never would have built Facebook. Movies and pop culture just get this all wrong. The idea of a single eureka moment is a dangerous lie. It makes us feel inadequate because we feel like we haven't had ours yet. And it prevents people with seeds of good ideas from ever getting started in the first place. It's really good to be idealistic, but be prepared to be misunderstood.

Anyone working on a big vision is going to get called crazy, even if you end up right. Anyone taking on a complex problem is going to get blamed for not fully understanding it, even though it's impossible to know everything up front. Anyone taking initiative will always get criticized for moving too fast, because there's always someone who wants to slow you down. In our society, we often don't take on big things because we're so afraid of making mistakes that we ignore all the things that are wrong today if we do nothing.

The reality is that anything we do today is going to have some issues in the future, but that can't stop us from getting started. So, what are we waiting for? It is time for our generation to define great work. Let's do big things, not just to create progress but to create purpose.

The second is redefining our idea of equality so everyone has the freedom to pursue their purpose. Facebook wasn't the first thing I built; I also built chat systems, games, study tools, and music players, and I'm not alone. J.K. Rowling got rejected 12 times before she finally wrote and published Harry Potter. The greatest successes come from having the freedom to fail.

I know a lot of entrepreneurs, and I don't know a single person who gave up on starting a business because they were worried that they might not make enough money. But I know too many people who haven't had the chance to pursue their dreams because they didn't have a cushion to fall back on if they failed. So many things go wrong when you start a business, and I think people frequently ask you, "What mistakes should you avoid making?" You know my answer to that question is: don't even bother trying to avoid mistakes, because you're going to make tons of them. And the important thing is actually learning quickly from whatever mistakes you make and not giving up. There are things every single year of Facebook's existence that could have killed us or made it so that it just seemed like moving forward and making a lot of progress just seemed intractable, but you just kind of bounce back and you learn that nothing is impossible and you just have to kind of keep running through the walls. It's just kind of hard; you need to be pretty headstrong about it.

There are going to be all these challenges that come up, and I think the main thing that you need to do is just not give up. The best entrepreneurs that I've met don't really start companies because their goal is not to build a company; they do it because they want to make a change in the world and help people, and if you kind of stay true to that and just focus on powering through no matter what the challenges are that will inevitably come up in your path, you'll find that there are lots of tools that are available and a lot of people who will help you build what you're building.

The third way we can create a sense of purpose for everyone is by building community. We understand that the great arc of human history bends toward people coming together in ever greater numbers. From tribes to cities to nations to achieve things that we could not do on our own. We get that our greatest opportunities are now global; we can be the generation that ends poverty and ends disease. Change begins locally; even global change begins with individuals such as ourselves. In our generation, the struggle of whether we connect more or whether we achieve our greatest opportunities comes down to this: your ability to build communities and create a world where every single person has a sense of purpose.

Finally, when faced with a significant challenge, Mark says, "May the source of strength who has blessed the ones before us help us find the courage to make our lives a blessing." I hope you will find the courage to make your life a blessing.

Break The Status Quo

I hope you've read everything in this book up to this point, so in the final chapter I'd like to recommend my points. I only have two things to say. Be curious and ask questions. The reason I say this is that if you do not ask questions, you will not get answers, and in order to ask those questions, you must be curious.

My life and mindset changed dramatically between the ages of 16 and 17 in comparison to previous years. If you ask me, what has been the most important period of your life up to this point? I consider this to be the most important period of my life, which began when I was 16. It was a time when I changed my mindset, learned a lot of new skills, tried new things, and, most importantly, became involved in entrepreneurship. When I was 17 years old, I realized, *"Everyone has two lives, and the second begins when you realize you only have one."* What I mean is that once you realize your time is limited, you will have numerous opportunities to do the things you've always wanted to do. Sure, you may have important periods in your life; all I ask is that you remember this.

Not only that, but I discovered how beautiful and challenging our lives can be. Many people wonder, "What is the purpose of life?" According to me, the purpose of life is to live. Whether you like it or not, you must turn every page of your life's book; you cannot skip any pages because everything is connected to where you are now. If you don't like your surroundings, work hard yourself to get out of it; if you don't like your current situation, work for yourself to get out of it; whatever you believe is possible.

When I see entrepreneurs and business people, I am inspired and respectful of them. They, like us, were born into a normal family, worked hard to overcome society's pressures, pursued their dreams, and were successful. This is not a simple matter.

So, after publishing this book, I put a lot of pressure on myself. Now I can't get away from anyone, not even my inner self. When I feel like I'm not pushing hard enough, I think about the stories and insights that I shared in this book. I overcome this by employing those goal-setting techniques mentioned in my book.

Maybe if I hadn't learned about these things in my life, I'd have followed the same path as everyone else. But all of this happened because I clicked on and watched that single YouTube video. When I first started pursuing entrepreneurship, my mind told me that there is no turning back; you can only move forward. There are only two options left. Option 1: Scared and quit with regret; Option 2: Make it a reality. I started to enjoy the progress I was making; there were ups and downs, but that was all part of the journey.

> *"Remember to look up the stars and not down at your feet. Try to make sense of what you see and wonder about what makes the universe exist. Be curious. And however life*

may seem, there is always something you can do and succeed at." – *Stephen Hawking*

Whenever I feel frustrated and overwhelmed, I simply see the stars in the sky because astronomy is my biggest stress buster. When you explore about astronomy you will know that we are just a dust in this universe. So, whenever you face problems in your life simply step into sometime on astronomy, you'll feel something great and unique about you.

When I learn new facts about our universe, it serves as a reminder that the challenges we face are insignificant in the grand scheme of things, and that we are only a small part of something much larger. There are an unimaginable number of stars, galaxies, and planets, and so many planets have life on them, you will feel something different when you start asking these questions.

"Reality is merely an illusion, albeit a very persistent one." – Albert Einstein

Everything is an illusion, including you and me. Our bodies have a finite lifespan, whereas the soul within them has an infinite age and life. So, an infinite thing combines with a finite thing to form what we call life. So, if everything is an illusion, what remains true?

- With this illusion, the impact you create is real.
- With this illusion, you are creating something true.
- With this illusion, you are changing people's lives, which is true, and thus the impact you create is real.

From now on, be adventurous, curious, ask questions, learn and try new things, and get out there and make an impact. Finally, realizing that your time is limited will help you live a far better life than others. This can also be expressed as the two most important days in your life: the day you were born and the day you find out why you were born.

My Recommended Reading

Rich Dad Poor Dad by Robert Kiyosaki

Rich Dad, Poor Dad is a personal finance classic that questions traditional thinking about money and investment. Kiyosaki teaches important lessons about financial literacy and mentality via the perspective of his own upbringing with two father figures: his biological father (poor dad) and his best friend's father (rich dad). Kiyosaki's clear writing style and practical counsel have made "Rich Dad Poor Dad" a timeless resource for anybody looking to reconsider their attitude to money and success.

The Almanack of Naval Ravikant: A Guide to Wealth and Happiness by Eric Jorgenson

The Almanack of Naval Ravikant is a selected compilation of wisdom and ideas from entrepreneur, investor, and philosopher Naval Ravikant. Eric Jorgenson compiled this book, which distills Ravikant's beliefs on life, happiness, prosperity, and success into a comprehensive roadmap for personal development and self-improvement. The Almanack draws on Ravikant's podcast interviews, tweets, and articles to provide practical guidance on issues like as decision-making, wealth creation, mentality, and spirituality. With its simple yet deep ideas, Naval Ravikant's Almanack provides a road map for leading a more meaningful and purposeful life.

Zero to One: Peter Thiel with Blake Masters

Zero to One, co-written by Peter Thiel and Blake Masters, is a breakthrough book that explores into the fundamentals of developing disruptive firms and driving innovation in today's society. Peter Thiel, a PayPal co-founder and early investor in firms such as Facebook, gives his thoughts on what it takes to get from zero—creating something wholly new—to one, gaining monopoly-like status in a market. This book contains vital lessons for budding entrepreneurs, business executives, and everyone interested in learning how to start genuinely innovative businesses.

Atomic Habits by James Clear

Atomic Habits is a revolutionary guide to developing and maintaining excellent habits for personal and professional development. James Clear provides a thorough framework for understanding the science of habit development, as well as practical tactics for making modest adjustments that yield big effects. With concrete guidance and real-life examples, "Atomic Habits" provides readers with the skills they need to develop long-term habits and achieve their goals consistently and easily.

***Think and Grow Rich* by** Napoleon Hill

Think and Grow Rich is a timeless classic that has motivated millions of people to succeed and flourish. Hill distills the elements of achievement into a strong philosophy of success using interviews with over 500 great people, including Andrew Carnegie, Thomas Edison, and Henry Ford. "Think and Grow Rich" offers readers a road map to realizing their full potential and fulfilling their ambitions via compelling stories and practical activities. Whether you're looking for riches, pleasure, or personal fulfilment, this book provides important insights into great achievers' mindsets and routines.

***How to Win Friends and Influence People* by** Dale Carnegie

How to Win Friends and Influence People is a guide to developing meaningful connections and achieving success in both your personal and professional life. Carnegie's principles, which are founded on decades of experience and study, highlight the significance of empathy, understanding, and communication in positively impacting people. From simple techniques for remembering names to strategies for resolving conflicts and persuading others to your point of view, "How to Win Friends and Influence People" provides timeless wisdom for anyone looking to improve their interpersonal skills and achieve their goals through the power of human connection.

The 7 Habits of Highly Effective People by Stephen R. Covey

The Seven Habits of Highly Effective People. is a groundbreaking self-help book that takes a comprehensive approach to personal and professional growth. Covey's concepts are centred on transforming one's thinking from dependency to independence, and eventually to interdependence, with an emphasis on effectiveness rather than efficiency. From proactivity and starting with the goal in mind to trying first to understand, then to be understood, Covey's paradigm gives a road map for attaining both success and fulfilment.

The Psychology of Money by Morgan Housel

The Psychology of Money is an engrossing examination of the intricate link between money and human behaviour. Housel digs into the psychological elements that influence our financial decisions, including the impact of emotions such as greed and fear, as well as the need of long-term planning and humility. Drawing on insights from psychology, history, and economics, he debunks prevalent wealth fallacies and provides practical guidance for sensible money management. With its combination of narrative and actionable ideas, this book gives readers a greater knowledge of the psychology of money and enables them to make better financial decisions for themselves and their future.

Steve Jobs by Walter Isaacson

Walter Isaacson's Steve Jobs is a thorough biography of one of the most important and mysterious people of the modern period. Isaacson provides readers with an intimate glimpse inside the life and thought of Apple Inc.'s co-founder, based on numerous interviews with Jobs himself as well as family members, acquaintances, and coworkers. Isaacson explore into Jobs' complicated personality, turbulent relationships, and unwavering determination to produce goods that are "insanely great." With its colourful storytelling and profound insights, "Steve Jobs" gives readers a better knowledge of the man behind the legendary computer business and the lessons to be learned from his amazing life. success.

Elon Musk by Walter Isaacson

Walter Isaacson's book Elon Musk explores deeply into the lives and accomplishments of one of our time's most innovative entrepreneurs. Isaacson dives into Musk's interesting life, from his infancy in South Africa to his rapid climb to the CEO of SpaceX and Tesla, among other companies. With its rich storytelling and intelligent analysis, "Elon Musk" gives readers a better knowledge of the man behind the breakthrough firms that are transforming industries and influencing humanity's future.

The Power of Your Subconscious Mind by Joseph Murphy

The Power of Your Subconscious Mind is a key text that examines the subconscious mind's enormous potential to influence our lives. Murphy shows readers how to reprogram their subconscious brains for success, health, and pleasure using a variety of practical strategies and exercises. Whether it's about conquering anxieties, strengthening relationships, or attracting riches, "The Power of Your Subconscious Mind" provides timeless wisdom and concrete ideas for anyone looking to harness the boundless potential of their mind to create the life they want.

Insights to Enhance Your Life by Jegadeesh S

Insights to Improve Your Life is a thought-provoking and practical guide to personal development and self-improvement. My friend wrote this book, which gives a fresh viewpoint on reaching your daily goals through his 100 life lessons. Jegadeesh provides wisdom obtained from personal experiences and observations in the form of insights, stories, and practical advice. With its realistic and inspirational sentiments, this book is guaranteed to encourage readers to go on their own journeys of self-discovery and personal growth.

Theory of Everything by Stephen Hawking

The Theory of Everything is a revolutionary investigation into basic concerns about physics and the nature of the cosmos. In this simple and interesting book, Hawking explains complicated scientific topics like general relativity and quantum physics in layman's terms. He explores issues ranging from the origins of the universe to the existence of black holes, providing insights into space, time, and the fundamental forces of the universe. Hawking's book encourages readers to consider the ultimate concerns of existence and provides a view into the cutting edge of current theoretical physics.

A Brief History of Time by Stephen Hawking

A Brief History of Time is a breathtaking overview of the cosmos and the rules that govern it. Hawking's internationally renowned book offers a thorough survey of contemporary cosmology, including the Big Bang hypothesis, black holes, and the structure of time itself. Despite dealing with complicated scientific issues, Hawking's language is understandable and fascinating, making the book appropriate for both scientists and casual readers. This book demonstrates not just Hawking's genius as a theoretical physicist, but also his ability to explain fundamental scientific concepts to a wide audience.

Brief Answers to the Big Questions by Stephen Hawking

This book provides a thought-provoking look at some of humanity's most urgent issues. In this posthumously released book, Hawking discusses complicated themes like as the existence of God, the future of artificial intelligence, and the feasibility of time travel, drawing on his experience as one of the world's most known theoretical physicists. With his trademark clarity and wit, Hawking pushes readers to address the universe's secrets and the difficulties that lie ahead. "Brief Answers to the Big Questions" demonstrates Hawking's continuing interest and dedication to furthering human understanding in the face of uncertainty.